Silverlight and ASP.NET Revealed

Matthew MacDonald

Silverlight and ASP.NET Revealed

Copyright © 2007 by Matthew MacDonald

ISBN-13 (pbk): 978-1-59059-939-6

ISBN-10 (pbk): 1-59059-939-X

eISBN-13: 978-1-4302-0543-2

Printed and bound in the United States of America (POD)

Lead Editor: Jonathan Hassell

Technical Reviewer: Stephen Kaufman

Editorial Board: Steve Anglin, Ewan Buckingham, Gary Cornell, Jason Gilmore, Jonathan Gennick, Jonathan Hassell, James Huddleston, Chris Mills, Matthew Moodie, Dominic Shakeshaft, Jim Sumser, Matt Wade
Project Manager: Denise Santoro Lincoln

Copy Edit Manager: Nicole Flores

Assistant Production Director: Kari Brooks-Copony

Compositor: Richard Ables

Cover Designer: Kurt Krames

Manufacturing Director: Tom Debolski

Distributed to the book trade worldwide by Springer-Verlag New York, Inc., 233 Spring Street, 6th Floor, New York, NY 10013. Phone 1-800-SPRINGER, fax 201-348-4505, e-mail orders-ny@springer-sbm.com, or visit http://www.springeronline.com.

For information on translations, please contact Apress directly at 2855 Telegraph Avenue, Suite 600, Berkeley, CA 94705. Phone 510-549-5930, fax 510-549-5939, e-mail info@apress.com, or visit http://www.apress.com.

The source code for this book is available to readers at http://www.apress.com in the Source Code/ Download section.

Contents

About the Author

MATTHEW MACDONALD is an author, educator, and MCSD developer who has a passion for emerging technologies. He is a regular writer for developer journals such as Inside Visual Basic, ASPToday, and Hardcore Visual Studio .NET, and he's the author of several books about programming with .NET, including *User Interfaces in VB .NET: Windows Forms and Custom Controls*, *The Book of VB .NET*, and *.NET Distributed Applications*. In a dimly remembered past life, he studied English literature and theoretical physics. Send e-mail to him with praise, condemnation, and everything in between, to p2p@prosetech.com.

Silverlight and ASP.NET Revealed

Although the Web is easily the most popular environment for business software, there are some things that web applications just can't do, or can't do very well. Even if you outfit your ASP.NET web pages with the latest cutting-edge JavaScript, you won't be able to duplicate many of the capabilities that desktop applications take for granted, such as animation, sound and video playback, and 3D graphics. And although you can use JavaScript to respond on the client to focus changes, mouse movements, and other "real-time" events, you still can't build a complex interface that's anywhere near as responsive as a window in a rich client application. (The saving grace of web programming is that you usually don't need these frills. The benefits you gain—broad compatibility, high security, no deployment cost, and a scalable server-side model—outweigh the loss of a few niceties.)

That said, developers are continuously pushing the limits of the Web. These days, it's not uncommon to watch an animated commercial or play a simple but richly designed game directly in your browser. This capability obviously isn't a part of the ordinary HTML, CSS, and JavaScript standards. Instead, it's enabled by a browser plug-in, sometimes for a Java applet, but most commonly for Flash content.

Microsoft's new Silverlight is a direct competitor to Flash. Like Flash, Silverlight allows you to create interactive content that runs on the client, with support for dynamic graphics, media, and animation that goes far beyond ordinary HTML. Also like Flash, Silverlight is deployed using a lightweight browser plug-in and supports a wide range of different browsers and operating systems. At the moment, Flash has the edge over Silverlight, because of its widespread adoption and its maturity. However, Silverlight boasts a few architectural features that Flash can't match—most importantly, the fact that it's based on a scaled-down version of .NET's common language runtime (CLR) and thus allows developers to write client-side code using pure C#.

Coming up, you'll take a detailed tour of Silverlight. You'll learn how it works, what features it supports, and what features aren't quite there yet. You'll also consider how you can use Silverlight to supplement ASP.NET websites, or even integrate Silverlight content into existing ASP.NET web pages.

Understanding Silverlight

Silverlight uses a familiar technique to go beyond the capabilities of standard web pages—it uses a lightweight browser plug-in.

The advantage of the plug-in model is that the user needs to install just a single component to see content created by a range of different people and companies. Installing the plug-in requires a small download and forces the user to confirm the operation in at least one security dialog box (and usually more). It takes a short but definite amount of time, and it's an inconvenience. However, once the plug-in is installed, the browser can process any content that uses the plug-in seamlessly, with no further prompting.

Figure 1 shows two views of a page with Silverlight content. On the left is the page you'll see if you *don't* have the Silverlight plug-in installed. At this point, you can click the Get Microsoft Silverlight picture to be taken to Microsoft's website, where you'll be prompted to install the plug-in and then sent back to the original page. On the right is the page you'll see once the Silverlight plug-in is installed.

▓**Note** Silverlight is designed to overcome the limitations of ordinary HTML to allow developers to create more graphical and interactive applications. However, Silverlight isn't a way for developers to break out of the browser's security sandbox. For the most part, Silverlight applications are limited in equivalent ways to ordinary web pages. For example, a Silverlight application is allowed to create and access files, but only those files that are stored in a special walled-off *isolated storage* area. Conceptually, isolated storage works like the cookies in an ordinary web page. Files are separated by website and the current user, and size is severely limited.

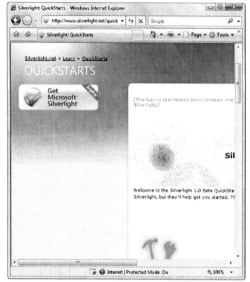 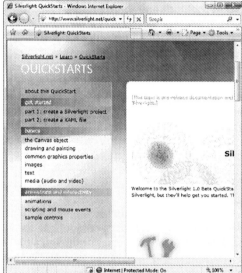

Figure 1. *Installing the Silverlight plug-in*

Silverlight vs. Flash

The most successful browser plug-in is Adobe Flash, which is installed on over 90 percent of the world's web browsers. Flash has a long history that spans more than ten years, beginning as a straightforward tool for adding animated graphics and gradually evolving into a platform for developing interactive content.

It's perfectly reasonable for ASP.NET developers to extend their websites using Flash content. However, doing so requires a separate design tool, and a completely different programming language (ActionScript) and programming environment (Flex). Furthermore, there's no straightforward way to generate Flash content user server-side .NET code, which means it's difficult to integrate ASP.NET content and Flash content—instead, they exist in separate islands.

▓**Note** There are some third-party solutions that help break down the barrier between ASP.NET and Flash. One example is the innovative SWFSource.NET (http://www.activehead.com/SWFSource.aspx), which provides a set of .NET classes that allow you to dynamically generate Flash (.swf) files. However, these tools work at a relatively low level. They fall far short of a full development platform.

Silverlight aims to give .NET developers a better option for creating rich web content. Silverlight provides a browser plug-in with many similar features to Flash, but one that's designed from the ground up for .NET. Silverlight natively supports the C# language and uses a range of .NET concepts. As a result, developers can write client-side code for Silverlight in the same language they use for server-side code (such as C# and VB), and use many of the same abstractions (including streams, controls, collections, generics, and LINQ).

The Silverlight plug-in has an impressive list of features, some of which are shared in common with Flash, and some which are entirely new and even revolutionary. They include the following:

- **Widespread browser support**: It's too early to tell how well the Silverlight browser works on different platforms. Currently, the beta builds of Silverlight 1.1 work on Windows Vista and Windows XP (in the PC universe) and OS X 10.4.8 or later (in the Mac world). The minimum browser versions that Silverlight 1.1 supports are Internet Explorer 6, Firefox 1.5.0.8, and Safari 2.0.4. Although Silverlight 1.1 doesn't currently work on Linux, the Mono team is creating an open-source Linux implementation of Silverlight 1.0 and Silverlight 1.1. This project is known as Moonlight, and it's being developed with key support from Microsoft. To learn more, visit http://www.mono-project.com/Moonlight.

- **Lightweight**: In order to encourage adoption, Silverlight is installed with a small-size setup (about 4 MB) that's easy to download. That allows it to provide an all-important "frictionless" setup experience, much like Flash (but quite different from Java).

- **2D Drawing**: Silverlight provides a rich model for 2D drawing. Best of all, the content you draw is defined as shapes and paths, so you can manipulate this content on the client side. You can even respond to events (like a mouse click on a portion of a graphic), which makes it easy to add interactivity to anything you draw.

- **Animation**: Silverlight has a time-based animation model that lets you define what should happen and how long it should take. The Silverlight plug-in handles the sticky details, like interpolating intermediary values and calculating the frame rate.

- **Media**: Silverlight provides playback of Windows Media Audio (WMA), Windows Media Video (WMV7–9), MP3 audio, and VC-1 (which supports high-definition). You aren't tied to the Windows Media Player ActiveX control or browser plug-in—instead, you can create any front-end you want, and you can even show video in full-screen mode. Microsoft also provides a free companion hosting service (at http://silverlight.live.com) that gives you 4 GB of space to store media files.

- **The CLR**: Most impressively, Silverlight includes a scaled-down version of the CLR, complete with an essential set of core classes, a garbage collector, a JIT (just-in-time) compiler, support for generics, and so on. In many cases, developers can take code written for the full .NET CLR and use it in a Silverlight application with only moderate changes.

- **Web service interaction**: Silverlight applications can call old-style ASP.NET web services (.asmx) or WCF (Windows Communication Foundation) web services. They can also send manually created XML requests over HTTP.

Of course, it's just as important to note what Silverlight *doesn't* include. Silverlight is a new technology that's evolving rapidly, and it's full of stumbling blocks for business developers who are used to relying on a rich library of prebuilt functionality. Not only does Silverlight lack any sort of data binding features, it also includes relatively few ready-made controls. Some basics, like buttons, are relatively easy to build yourself. But others, like text boxes, are not.

At present, Silverlight is primarily of interest to developers who plan to create a highly graphical, complete customized user interface, and who aren't afraid to perform a fair bit of work.

Silverlight Adoption

Silverlight is *very* new—so new that at the time of this writing, it exists in two versions (1.0 and 1.1), both of which are only available in beta form. For that reason, it's difficult to predict how well Silverlight will stack up against Flash's real strength: adoption.

At present, Silverlight is only on a fraction of computers. However, Microsoft is convinced that if compelling content exists for Silverlight, users will download the plug-in. There are a number of factors that support this argument. Flash grew dramatically in a short space of time, and Microsoft has obvious experience with other web-based applications that have started small and eventually gained wide adoption. (Windows Messenger comes to mind, along with numerous ActiveX plug-ins for tasks ranging from multiuser coordination on MSN Games to Windows verification on MSDN.)

A key point to keep in mind when considering the Silverlight development model is that in most cases you'll use Silverlight to *augment* the existing content of your website (which is still based on HTML, CSS, and JavaScript). For example, you might add Silverlight content that shows an advertisement or allows an enhanced experience for a portion of a website (such as playing a game, completing a survey, interacting with a product, taking a virtual tour, and so on). Your Silverlight pages may present content that's already available in your website in a more engaging way, or they may represent a value-added feature for users who have the Silverlight plug-in.

Although, it's easily possible to create a Silverlight-only website, it's unlikely that you'll take that approach. The fact that Silverlight is still relatively new, and the fact that it doesn't support legacy clients (most notably, it has no support for users of Windows ME, Windows 2000, and Windows 98) mean it doesn't have nearly the same reach as ordinary HTML. Many businesses that are adopting Silverlight are using it to distinguish themselves from other online competitors with cutting-edge content.

SILVERLIGHT 1.0 AND 1.1

Silverlight exists in two versions:

- The first version, Silverlight 1.0, is a relatively modest technology. It includes the 2D drawing features and the media playback features. However, it doesn't include the CLR engine or support for .NET languages, so any code you write must use JavaScript.

- The second version, Silverlight 1.1, adds the .NET-powered features that have generated the most developer excitement. It includes the CLR, a subset of .NET Framework classes, and a user interface model based on WPF (as described in the next section, "Silverlight and WPF").

Although Silverlight 1.1 is the least mature of the two, it's the one that has the most appeal for .NET developers. Here we're focusing on Silverlight 1.1.

Silverlight and WPF

One of the most interesting aspects of Silverlight is the fact that it borrows the WPF (Windows Presentation Foundation) model for designing rich, client-side user interfaces.

WPF is a recently introduced, next-generation technology for creating Windows applications that has built-in support for rich features like 3D graphics, animation, document display, and much more. It was introduced in .NET 3.0 as the successor to Windows Forms. WPF is notable because it not only simplifies development with a powerful set of high-level features, it also increases performance by rendering everything through the DirectX pipeline. To learn about WPF, you can refer to *Pro WPF: Windows Presentation Foundation in .NET 3.0* (Apress).

Silverlight obviously can't duplicate the features of WPF, because many of them rely deeply on the capabilities of the operating system, including Windows-specific display drivers and DirectX technology. However, rather than invent an entirely new set of controls and classes for client-side development, Silverlight uses a subset of the WPF model. If you've had any experience with WPF, you'll be surprised to see how closely Silverlight resembles its bigger brother. Here are a few common details:

- To define a Silverlight user interface (the collection of elements that makes up a Silverlight page or content window), you use XAML markup, just as you do with WPF.

Note XAML (short for Extensible Application Markup Language, and pronounced *zammel*) is a markup language used to instantiate .NET objects. Coming up, you'll see how it's used to define Silverlight content.

- When creating your user interface, you use elements that are also found in WPF, including the Canvas layout container; shapes like the Rectangle, Ellipse, Line, Polyline, and Polygon; the TextBlock and Image; and so on.

Note In WPF terminology, each graphical widget that appears in a user interface and is represented by a .NET class is called an *element*. The term *control* is generally reserved for elements that allow user interaction.

- To draw 2D graphics in Silverlight, you use paths, transforms, geometries, and brushes, all of which closely match their WPF equivalents.
- Silverlight provides a declarative animation model that's based on storyboards, and works in the same way as WPF's animation system.
- To show video or play audio files, you use the MediaElement class, as you do in WPF.

Microsoft has made no secret about its intention to continue to expand the capabilities of Silverlight by drawing from the full WPF model. In future Silverlight releases, you're likely to see features like data binding, more layout containers, elements that duplicate common Windows controls, and so on.

In other words, Silverlight is a .NET-based Flash competitor. It aims to compete with Flash today, but provide a path to far more features in the future. Unlike the Flash development model, which is limited in several ways due to the way it's evolved over the years, Silverlight is a starting-from-scratch attempt that's thoroughly based on .NET and WPF, and will therefore allow .NET developers to be far more productive. In many ways, Silverlight is the culmination of two trends: the drive to extend web pages to incorporate more and more rich client features, and the drive to give the .NET Framework a broader reach.

Installing Silverlight and the Visual Studio Extensions

Although you could create a Silverlight page by hand, it's not easy (and not worth the trouble). Instead, it makes sense to use a design tool like Visual Studio or Expression Blend.

Currently, Visual Studio doesn't have design-time support for creating Silverlight content. However, Microsoft has released a free add-in with extensions for developing Silverlight 1.1 content in Visual Studio 2008. These extensions, which are in beta at the time of this writing, include helpful templates for creating websites and ASP.NET pages that use Silverlight content. However, these extensions currently don't include a visual designer. In other words, there's no way to view your Silverlight content in Visual Studio or drag and drop it into existence. Instead, you'll need to code the markup by hand and then run it in a browser.

You can download the Visual Studio extensions and everything else you need to started with Silverlight from http://silverlight.net/GetStarted. Here's what you'll find:

- **The Silverlight 1.1 runtime**: This is the browser plug-in that allows you to run Silverlight content. (You'll also see the Silverlight 1.0 runtime, which is completely separate.)

- **ASP.NET Futures**: This is an add-on to ASP.NET that includes features that will be a part of future ASP.NET releases. (Of course, these features may change quite a bit by the time they make it into an official release. ASP.NET AJAX is an example of a technology that was released first as a separate add-on, and then integrated into the .NET Framework.) ASP.NET Futures includes the Xaml web control, which is a requirement if you want a straightforward way to place Silverlight content into a region of an ASP.NET page.

- **Silverlight Tools for Visual Studio 2008**: This is the Visual Studio add-in that allows you to create Silverlight websites and Silverlight pages for use with the Xaml web control.

- **The Silverlight 1.1 Software Development Kit**: This SDK provides additional documentation and samples. It's optional, but useful.

Before you continue to the Silverlight samples, make sure you've installed all these components: the Silverlight 1.1 runtime, ASP.NET Futures, and Silverlight Tools for Visual Studio.

Future versions of Visual Studio are sure to offer better design-time support for Silverlight content. There's also one other option—you can create Silverlight applications using Microsoft Expression Blend 2, a professional design tool that has many of the capabilities of Visual Studio, but is intended for UI designers and highly graphics-oriented development (rather than pure coding). Expression Blend 2 allows you to create desktop applications that use WPF and web pages that use Silverlight, but it doesn't allow you to create ASP.NET web pages. Thus, if you use Expression Blend 2, it's up to you to create the ASP.NET web pages for the rest of your site in Visual Studio.

Expression Blend 2 is currently in an early beta stage, and it isn't discussed here. However, you can find entire books about Expression Blend 1, which allows you to create full-fledged WPF user interfaces (but not Silverlight content) using the same model.

Creating a Silverlight Project

There are two ways to integrate Silverlight content into an ASP.NET application:

- **Create HTML files with Silverlight content**: You place these files in your ASP.NET website folder, just as you would with any other ordinary HTML file. The only limitation of this approach is that your HTML file obviously can't include ASP.NET controls, because it won't be processed on the server.

- **Place Silverlight content inside an ASP.NET web form**: To pull this trick off, you need the help of the Xaml web control. You can also add other ASP.NET controls to different regions of the page. The only disadvantage to this approach is that the page is always processed on the server. If you aren't actually using any server-side ASP.NET content, this creates an extra bit of overhead that you don't need when the page is first requested.

Of course, you're also free to mingle both of these approaches, and use Silverlight content in dedicated HTML pages and inside ASP.NET web pages in the same site.

Visual Studio provides two ways to develop Silverlight content, which almost (but don't quite) line up:

- **Create a Silverlight project**: A Silverlight project consists of Silverlight files (XAML files that define your Silverlight content and code, and ordinary HTML web pages that expose this content. Because Silverlight is a client-side technology, you can request these HTML pages directly in your web browser. Visual Studio doesn't need to use its integrated web server, because there's no code running on the server.

- **Use the Xaml control in an ASP.NET web form**: You can use the Xaml control in an existing ASP.NET web form in an existing ASP.NET website. The Xaml web control is an ASP.NET web control with a difference—instead of rendering the usual HTML and JavaScript, it renders the XAML markup that defines a Silverlight user interface. However, the XAML markup isn't coded directly in your ASP.NET page (which would be a bit messy). Instead, it's pulled out of a separate Silverlight file that's a part of your website.

In this section, you'll begin by using the first approach. After you've explored the Silverlight environment and you've seen how to integrate Silverlight content into ordinary web pages, you'll consider how you can embed it in an ASP.NET web form.

To create a Silverlight project, simply select File ➤ New ➤ Project in Visual Studio and select the Silverlight Project template. As usual, you need to pick a project name and a location on your hard drive before clicking OK to create the project.

Every Silverlight project starts with a small set of essential files, as shown in Figure 2. These files are described in the following sections.

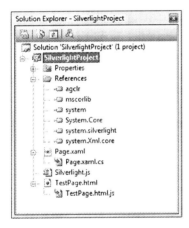

Figure 2. *A Silverlight project*

The HTML Entry Page

This page is the entry point into your Silverlight content—in other words, the page the user requests in the web browser. Visual Studio names this file TestPage.html, although you'll probably want to rename it to something more appropriate.

The HTML entry page doesn't actually *contain* the Silverlight markup or code-behind. Instead, it creates it using a small amount of JavaScript. (For this reason, browsers that have JavaScript disabled won't be able to see Silverlight content.)

Here's what the HTML entry page looks like:

```
<html xmlns="http://www.w3.org/1999/xhtml">
<head>
    <title>Silverlight Project Test Page </title>
    <script type="text/javascript" src="Silverlight.js"></script>
    <script type="text/javascript" src="TestPage.html.js"></script>
    <style type="text/css">
        .silverlightHost { width: 640px; height: 480px; }
    </style>
</head>

<body>
    <div id="SilverlightControlHost" class="silverlightHost">
        <script type="text/javascript">
            createSilverlight();
        </script>
    </div>
</body>
</html>
```

As you can see, this page references two other JavaScript files (TestPage.html.js and Silverlight.js). Although you could add other HTML content to the page, this example includes a single <div> element where the Silverlight control will be placed. When this <div> element is processed, the JavaScript code in the script block is executed. This code calls the createSilverlight() function (which is defined in TestPage.html.js) to generate the Silverlight content. After the content has been created and the browser has processed all the markup in the HTML entry page, the onload event of the body element ensures that the SilverlightControl gets the keyboard focus.

Note Visual Studio sets TestPage.html to be the start page for your project. As a result, when you launch your project, this page will be loaded in the browser. You can choose a different start page by right-clicking an HTML file in the Solution Explorer and choosing Set As Start Page.

The Silverlight Initialization Script

By default, Visual Studio generates a JavaScript function named createSilverlight() to initialize your Silverlight content region. It places this code in a file named TestPage.html.js (although you're free to rename the file or move the JavaScript code elsewhere, so long as you update the references in the HTML entry page to match).

Here's what the createSilverlight() function looks like:

```
function createSilverlight()
{
    Silverlight.createObjectEx({
      source: "Page.xaml",
      parentElement: document.getElementById("SilverlightControlHost"),
      id: "SilverlightControl",
        properties: {
          width: "100%",
          height: "100%",
          version: "1.1",
```

```
        enableHtmlAccess: "true"
      },
    events: {}
  });

  // Give the keyboard focus to the Silverlight control by default
  document.body.onload = function() {
    var silverlightControl = document.getElementById('SilverlightControl');
    if (silverlightControl)
    silverlightControl.focus();
  }
}
```

The createSilverlight() function calls the Sys.Silverlight.createObjectEx() function, which is defined in the Silverlight.js file. The Silverlight.js file is a basic piece of Silverlight infrastructure, and one you're not likely to modify. It includes the JavaScript that checks if Silverlight is installed (and offers to redirect the user if it's not) and the JavaScript that instantiates the Silverlight control. If you have several Silverlight applications on the same web server, they might well use the same Silverlight.js file.

On the other hand, the code in the createSilverlight() function in the TestPage.html.js file is more significant. When the createSilverlight() function calls createObjectEx(), it specifies a few key details about the Silverlight control, including the name of the XAML file where the markup is stored, the name of the <div> element where the Silverlight control will be placed, the name that will be assigned to the Silverlight control, the size of the Silverlight control, the minimum required Silverlight version, and whether you want to enable interaction between Silverlight and the HTML DOM. Because this information varies, every Silverlight page has its own createSilverlight() function to set up the Silverlight content region.

In this example (which shows the default code generated by Visual Studio), the XAML file is named Page.xaml, the <div> element is named SilverlightControlHost, and the Silverlight control will be named SilverlightControl.

The width and height are set to 100%, which means the Silverlight content will always be just large enough to fill the containing element. In this case, the element is a <div> element that's placed directly in the body of your web page. Ordinarily, a <div> element placed in this way is allowed to grow without restriction. However, when you create a Silverlight page, Visual Studio adds a style rule that limits the size of the <div>. The style rule looks like this:

```
<style type="text/css">
  .silverlightHost { width: 640px; height: 480px; }
</style>
```

This gives the <div> element an exact size of 640✕480 pixels. You can alter the style rule to choose a different size. (You could also change the parameters in the createObjectEx() call so that they use fixed pixel values, but it's clearer to place these details in the HTML file.)

You can remove the height property so the Silverlight content region expands to fit the available width but is limited in size. If you remove both the width and height properties (or remove the style rule altogether), the Silverlight content region will be sized to fit its container, which in this case gives it the height and width of the browser window. This usually won't be the behavior you want, and it's definitely not the right choice if you have other HTML content on the page. (For example, if you have some HTML content after your <div> element, this content won't be visible, because it will always remain just underneath the Silverlight content, which fills the browser window.) If you don't use the width and height properties, you'll probably want to constrain the <div> element by placing it in a specific place in your layout, such as in between other <div> elements, in another fixed-size element, or in a cell in a table.

Tip You can also apply a <div> style to draw a border around your Silverlight content region, so you can clearly see its bounds. To do so, simply set the CSS border properties in the style.

After the width and height information are two more details in the createObjectEx() call. The version indicates the minimum required version of Silverlight that the client must have installed in order to see this content. If the version doesn't match, the user will be prompted to install the appropriate version of Silverlight from Microsoft's website.

Finally, the last property that you pass to createObjectEx() is the enableHtmlAccess flag. Use true if you want to be able to interact with the HTML elements on the entry page through your Silverlight code. You'll learn how to take this step later on.

The XAML Page

When your entry page calls createObjectEx(), it specifies the name of a XAML file. This XAML file contains the markup that's used to generate the set of elements that appears in the Silverlight content region. By default, Visual Studio names this file Page.xaml.

Here's the markup that Visual Studio adds to the Page.xaml file, with one added line—the <TextBlock> element that's highlighted in bold:

```
<Canvas x:Name="parentCanvas"
  xmlns="http://schemas.microsoft.com/client/2007"
  xmlns:x="http://schemas.microsoft.com/winfx/2006/xaml"
  Loaded="Page_Loaded"
  x:Class="SilverlightProject1.Page;assembly=ClientBin/SilverlightProject1.dll"
  Width="640"
  Height="480"
  Background="White"
>
  <TextBlock FontSize="20">Hello, World!</TextBlock>
</Canvas>
```

This gives you enough to test your Silverlight project. If you run your application, Visual Studio launches your default web browser and navigates to TestPage.html. The test page creates a new Silverlight control and initializes it using the markup in Page.xaml. Figure 3 shows the modest final result.

Figure 3. *A page with Silverlight content*

In order to understand how this markup works and how to create the Silverlight user interface you want, you need to dig deeper into the XAML standard.

Understanding XAML

XAML is a markup language used to instantiate .NET objects. Although XAML is a technology that can be applied to many different problem domains, it was primarily designed as a way for developers to construct WPF user interfaces for rich Windows applications. As Silverlight is a small subset of WPF, it uses the same XAML markup standard.

Conceptually, XAML plays an analogous role to HTML. HTML allows you to define the elements that make up an ordinary web page. XAML allows you to define the elements that make up a block of XAML content. To manipulate HTML elements, you use client-side JavaScript (or just rerender the entire page, as ASP.NET does after every postback). To manipulate XAML elements, you write client-side C# code. Finally, both XAML and HTML look the same. Like XHTML, XAML is an XML-based language that consists of elements that can be nested in any arrangement you like to express containment.

You can write XAML markup by hand, or you can use a tool that generates the XAML you need. Currently, Visual Studio does not include support for creating XAML pages with a visual design surface, although you can expect it to appear soon (after all, Visual Studio *does* allow you to design XAML windows for a full-fledged WPF application).

Silverlight Elements

Every element in a XAML document maps to an instance of a Silverlight class. The name of the element matches the name of the class *exactly*. For example, the element <Canvas> instructs Silverlight to create a Canvas object. <TextBlock> instructs Silverlight to create a TextBlock object. Because the <TextBlock> element is nested inside the <Canvas> element, and because the Canvas is a container control, the TextBlock is placed inside the Canvas.

Currently, Silverlight includes a very small set of elements, as described in Table 1. Many more are expected in future builds. You'll encounter all of these elements as you continue.

Table 1. *Silverlight Elements*

Class	Description
Canvas	A layout container that can hold any number of other Silverlight elements, arranged with fixed coordinates.
TextBlock	An element that contains single-line or multiline text content.
Image	An element that shows a picture file, typically using the GIF, JPG, or PNG format.
Rectangle, Ellipse, Line, Polygon, Polyline, Path	Shape drawing elements that represent various 2D figures. You can use these in combination to build up a complex piece of vector art.
MediaElement	An element that manages the playback of an audio or video file and, optionally, displays a video window.

XAML Namespaces

When you use an element like <Canvas> in a XAML file, the Silverlight parser recognizes that you want to create an instance of the Canvas class. However, it doesn't necessarily know *what* Canvas class to use. After all, even if the Silverlight namespaces only include a single class with that name, there's no guarantee that you won't create a similarly named class of your own. Clearly, you need a way to indicate the Silverlight namespace information in order to use an element.

In Silverlight, classes are resolved by mapping XML namespaces to Silverlight namespaces. In the sample document shown earlier, two namespaces are defined:

```
<Canvas x:Name="parentCanvas"
  xmlns="http://schemas.microsoft.com/client/2007"
  xmlns:x="http://schemas.microsoft.com/winfx/2006/xaml"
```

You'll find these two namespaces in every XAML document you create for Silverlight:

- http://schemas.microsoft.com/client/2007 is the core Silverlight 1.1 namespace. It encompasses all the Silverlight 1.1 classes, including the Canvas. Ordinarily, this namespace is declared without a namespace prefix, so it becomes the default namespace for the entire document. In other words, every element is automatically placed in this namespace unless you specify otherwise.

- http://schemas.microsoft.com/winfx/2006/xaml is the XAML namespace. It includes various XAML utility features that allow you to influence how your document is interpreted. This namespace is mapped to the prefix *x*.

In many situations, you'll want to have access to your own namespaces in a XAML file. The most common example is if you want to use a custom Silverlight control that you (or another developer) have created. In this case, you need to define a new XML namespace prefix and map it to your assembly. Here's the syntax you need:

```
<Canvas x:Name="parentCanvas"
  xmlns:w="clr-namespace:Widgets;assembly=ClientBin/Widgets.dll"
  ...
```

The XML namespace declaration sets three pieces of information:

- **The XML namespace prefix:** You'll use the namespace prefix to refer to the namespace in your XAML page. In this example, that's *w*, although you can choose anything you want that doesn't conflict with another namespace prefix.

- **The .NET namespace:** In this case, the classes are located in the Widgets namespace. If you have classes that you want to use in multiple namespaces, you can map them to different XML namespaces or to the same XML namespace (as long as there aren't any conflicting class names).

- **The assembly:** In this case, the classes are part of the Widgets.dll assembly. You always precede this assembly with the folder name ClientBin. This is the subfolder of your website where Visual Studio places your compiled Silverlight assembly and any class library assemblies that it uses. (You'll consider the Silverlight compilation model in more detail a bit later on) If you want to use a class that's defined in your Silverlight project assembly, the assembly name is based on the name of your project, as in SilverlightProject1.dll.

▓**Note** Remember, Silverlight uses a lean, stripped-down version of the CLR. For that reason, a Silverlight application can't use a full .NET class library assembly. Instead, it needs to use a Silverlight class library. You can easily create a Silverlight class library in Visual Studio by choosing the Silverlight Class Library project template.

Once you've mapped your .NET namespace to an XML namespace, you can use it anywhere in your XAML document. For example, if the Widgets namespace contains a control named HotButton, you could create an instance like this:

```
<w:HotButton Text="Click Me!" Click="DoSomething"></w:HotButton>
```

The XAML Code-Behind

XAML allows you to construct a user interface, but in order to make a functioning application, you need a way to connect the event handlers that have your application code. XAML makes this easy using the Class attribute shown here:

```
<Canvas x:Name="parentCanvas" ...
  x:Class="SilverlightProject1.Page;assembly=ClientBin/SilverlightProject1.dll"
  ...
```

The *x* namespace prefix places the Class attribute in the XAML namespace, which means the Class attribute is a more general part of the XAML language, not a specific Silverlight ingredient.

In fact, the Class attribute tells the Silverlight parser to generate a new class with the specified name. That class derives from the class that's named by the XML element. In other words, this example creates a new class named SilverlightProject1.Page, which derives from the base Canvas class. The automatically generated portion of this class is merged with the code you've supplied in the code-behind file.

Usually, every XAML file will have a corresponding code-behind class with client-side C# code. Visual Studio creates a code-behind class for the Page.xaml file named Page.xaml.cs. Here's what you'll see in the Page.xaml.cs file:

```
using System;
using System.Windows;
using System.Windows.Controls;
using System.Windows.Documents;
using System.Windows.Ink;
using System.Windows.Input;
using System.Windows.Media;
using System.Windows.Media.Animation;
using System.Windows.Shapes;

namespace SilverlightProject1
{
    public partial class Page : Canvas
    {
        private void Page_Loaded(object o, EventArgs e)
        {
            // Required to initialize variables
            InitializeComponent();
        }
    }
}
```

Keen eyes will notice that the Page_Loaded() event handler actually responds to an event with a slightly different name—the Canvas.Loaded event. The event handler is attached in the XAML markup for the page. The name Page_Loaded() is used because it's more familiar to ASP.NET developers, and it more clearly communicates what's just taken place—namely, the Silverlight content on the page has finished being initialized.

Currently, the Page class code doesn't include any real functionality. However, it does include one important detail—the default constructor, which calls InitializeComponent() when you create an instance of the class. This parses your markup, creates the corresponding objects, sets their properties, and attaches any event handlers you've defined.

Note   The InitializeComponent() method plays a key role in Silverlight content. For that reason, you should never delete the InitializeComponent() call from the constructor. Similarly, if you add another constructor, make sure it also calls InitializeComponent().

There's one more detail to consider. In your code-behind class, you'll often want to manipulate controls programmatically. For example, you might want to read or change properties or attach and detach event handlers on the fly. To make this possible, the control must include the Name attribute. In the previous example, the TextBlock control does not include a Name attribute, so you won't be able to manipulate it in your code-behind file.

Here's how you can attach a name to the TextBlock:

```
<TextBlock x:Name="txt" FontSize="20">Hello, World!</TextBlock>
```

This model is surprisingly like developing an ASP.NET web page. However, the underlying plumbing is completely different. XAML markup is parsed on the client side by the Silverlight engine using a scaled-down version of the CLR. The final content is rendered using a specialized Silverlight control that's embedded in the page. ASP.NET markup is processed by the ASP.NET engine on the server, along with any ordinary HTML that the page contains. The final result is rendered to HTML and then sent to the client.

Properties and Events

In order to do anything practical with Silverlight, you need to set the properties of your elements and attach event handlers to their events.

Setting properties is straightforward—you simply use an attribute with the value as a string. Silverlight uses type converters (as in ASP.NET pages) to convert the string value to the appropriate data type. In many cases, this is an easy task—for example, there's no difficulty in changing a string with a number into a number or a string with a color name into the corresponding color value. However, in other situations you need to set a property using an object that can't be easily represented as a single string.

In Silverlight, this is handled with a special nested element syntax. The nested element takes a two-part name in the form ClassName.PropertyName. Inside this element, you can instantiate the object you want with the appropriate element.

For example, the following markup sets the Canvas.Background property by creating a RadialGradientBrush. It does this using a <Canvas.Background> element (rather than setting the Background attribute of the <Canvas> element, as in the previous examples.) To configure the RadialGradientBrush, you need to supply a center point for the gradient, and the gradient stops (the colors in the gradient). Figure 4 shows the result.

```
<Canvas ... >
  <Canvas.Background>
    <RadialGradientBrush Center="0.5,0.5">
      <GradientStop Offset="0" Color="LightSteelBlue" />
      <GradientStop Offset="1" Color="White" />
    </RadialGradientBrush>
  </Canvas.Background>
```

```
   <TextBlock x:Name="txt" FontSize="20">Hello, World!</TextBlock>
</Canvas>
```

Figure 4. *A Canvas with a RadialGradientBrush background*

To attach an event, you also use attributes. However, now you need to assign the name of your event handler to the name of the event. This is similar to the approach used in ASP.NET web pages, except for that fact that event attributes do not begin with the word On.

Silverlight elements support a relatively small set of events, including GotFocus, KeyDown, KeyUp, Loaded, LostFocus, MouseEnter, MouseLeave, MouseLeftButtonDown, MouseLeftButtonUp, and MouseMove. There is no higher-level Click event.

For example, here's an event handler that responds to a mouse click by altering the text in the TextBlock:

```
public partial class Page : Canvas
{
    ...

    private void txt_Click(object o, EventArgs e)
    {
        txt.Text = "You clicked here.";
    }
}
```

And here's how you can wire that event up to the TextBlock:

```
<TextBlock ... MouseLeftButtonDown="txt_Click">Hello, World!</TextBlock>
```

Silverlight Compilation

Because Silverlight uses the CLR (albeit a pared-down, streamlined version), it supports the same compilation model as other .NET applications.

When you build your Silverlight application, the code is compiled to an assembly that's named after your project (for example, SilverlightProject1.dll). This assembly is the ClientBin subfolder inside your project directory. Unlike the code in ASP.NET web applications, the code in a Silverlight project must be compiled during development—the server does not perform JIT compilation when a Silverlight file is requested. This makes sense—after all, there's no reason to assume the web server for a Silverlight application even has the .NET Framework installed.

The Silverlight project assembly contains the code from your code-behind classes, and the compiled code for any other code files in your project. Optionally, it can also include resources—binary blocks of data that need to be easily accessible, such as images. Although these resources *could* include XAML documents that are extracted using code, in the present Visual Studio development model the XAML files you create aren't embedded in the assembly. (Developers who create custom Silverlight controls often use this model, and embed the XAML templates that define their control content as an assembly resource.)

The Silverlight compilation model has a number of advantages, including easy deployment and vastly improved performance when compared to ordinary JavaScript. However, although the code is compiled, the same considerations apply to Silverlight assemblies as any other type of client-side code. IL code can be easily decompiled or reverse engineered, so it's not an appropriate place to store secrets (like encryption keys, proprietary algorithms, and so on). If you need to perform a task that uses sensitive code, consider calling a web service from your Silverlight application.

Once you understand the Silverlight compilation model, it's a short step to understanding the deployment model. When you deploy a Silverlight application, you need to transfer the following files to the web server:

- The HTML entry pages.
- The .js script pages.
- The XAML pages.
- The ClientBin folder, with all its assemblies. (You don't need the .pdb debugging files.)

You don't need to copy the raw source code, because it's compiled into the project assembly in the ClientBin folder.

When hosting a Silverlight application, your web server must be configured to allow requests for two new file types: .xaml and .dll. This allows the HTML entry page to download the initial XAML page, which then in turn downloads the project assembly that contains the code-behind class.

The Silverlight execution model is quite straightforward. First, the client requests the HTML entry page. At this point, the browser downloads the HTML file and the linked .js file. While processing the HTML page, the browser executes the JavaScript code, including the createObjectEx() call that creates the Silverlight content region. After this step, the client-side plug-in takes over. It downloads the linked XAML file (which is identified by the source parameter that's passed to the createObjectEx() method). As the plug-in processes the XAML file, it comes across the Class attribute, which references the compiled project assembly. The browser then downloads that assembly in its entirety, along with any other referenced assemblies (such as class library assemblies that contain your own custom types and are used in the page). These assemblies are cached on the client side, so they don't need to be repeatedly downloaded each time the user visits a new page that uses the same assembly. All the Silverlight code is executed on the client side by the scaled down version of the .NET Framework that's embedded in the Silverlight plug-in.

Silverlight Essentials

Now that you've had an overview of the Silverlight model, you're ready to take a closer look at the fundamental concepts that go into building Silverlight content. In this section, you'll explore the Silverlight version of the .NET Framework, the Silverlight layout model, and the TextBlock. You'll also learn how to interact with HTML elements and use isolated storage.

.NET Framework Classes in Silverlight

Silverlight includes a subset of the classes from the full .NET Framework. Although it would be impossible to cram the entire .NET Framework into Silverlight—after all, it's a 4 MB download that needs to support a variety of browsers and operating systems—Silverlight includes a remarkable amount.

The Silverlight version of the .NET Framework is simplified in two ways. First, it doesn't provide the sheer number of types you'll find in the full .NET Framework. Second, the classes that it does include often don't provide the full complement of constructors, methods, properties, and events. Instead, Silverlight keeps only the most practical members of the most important classes, which leaves it with enough functionality to create surprisingly compelling code.

Note The Silverlight classes are designed to have public interfaces that resemble their full-fledged counterparts in the .NET Framework. However, the actual plumbing of these classes is quite different. All the Silverlight classes have been rewritten from the ground up to be as streamlined and efficient as possible.

Before you start doing any serious Silverlight programming, you might like to browse the Silverlight version of the .NET Framework. One way to do so is to open a Silverlight project, and then show the Object Browser in Visual Studio (choose View ➤ Object Browser). Along with the assembly for the code in your project, you'll see the following Silverlight assemblies (shown in Figure 5):

- **mscorlib.dll**: This assembly is the Silverlight equivalent of the mscorlib.dll assembly that includes the most fundamental parts of the .NET Framework. The Silverlight version includes core data types, exceptions, and interfaces in the System namespace, ordinary and generic collections, file management classes, and support for globalization, reflection, resources, debugging, and multithreading.

Note Some of the members in the Silverlight assemblies are only available to .NET Framework code, and aren't callable from your code. These members are marked with the SecurityCritical attribute. However, this attribute does not appear in the Object Browser, so you won't be able to determine whether a specific feature is usable in a Silverlight application until you try to use it. (If you attempt to use a member that has the SecurityCritical attribute, you'll get a SecurityException.) For example, Silverlight applications are only allowed to access the file system through the isolated storage API. For that reason, the constructor for the FileStream class is decorated with the SecurityCritical attribute.

- **System.dll**: This assembly contains additional generic collections, classes for dealing with URIs, and classes for dealing with regular expressions.

- **System.Core.dll**: This assembly contains support for LINQ. (You may remember that all the features that are new to .NET 3.5 are implemented in an assembly named System.Core.dll.)

- **System.Silverlight.dll**: This assembly contains classes for interacting with HTML elements, a version of the OpenFileDialog that works with isolated storage, and classes for sending HTTP requests.

- **System.Xml.core.dll**: This assembly includes the bare minimum classes you need for XML processing: XmlReader and XmlWriter.

- **agclr.dll**: This assembly includes the Silverlight UI classes that have been derived from the WPF model. For example, you'll find classes for all the Silverlight elements and for animation. (It's rumored that the *ag* in the name agclr.dll is derived from the symbol for Silver in the periodic table, while *clr* represents the scaled-down version of the CLR that Silverlight uses.)

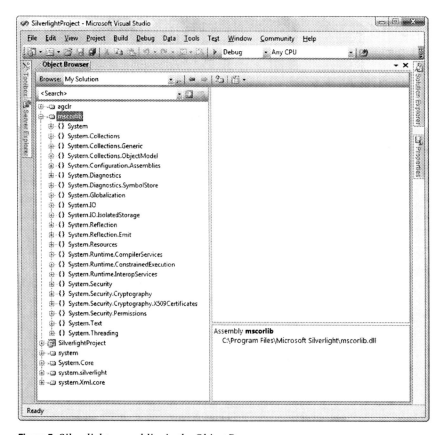

Figure 5. *Silverlight assemblies in the Object Browser*

The Canvas

In the example you considered in the previous section, the root element in the XAML page was a Canvas.

The Canvas is a *layout container*, which means it's an element that holds (and displays) other elements. The full WPF platform includes several layout managers, including ones that automatically stack elements, wrap them over multiple lines, or arrange them into an invisible grid. The Canvas is the simplest layout manager—it simply positions each item using fixed coordinates. Although more layout managers are planned for Silverlight, the Canvas is the only one that's currently included.

Technically, you can use any element as the root of a Silverlight XAML file. However, the Canvas is the most common and logical choice because of its ability to hold other elements. For example, if you use a Rectangle as the root element, your Silverlight content will be limited to that single Rectangle object, because the Rectangle can't hold anything else inside.

Note By default, Visual Studio sets the size of the Canvas to 640×480 by setting the Width and Height properties in the XAML file. However, there's a potential discrepancy at work because the content inside the Canvas is allowed to overflow its bounds. Thus, if you place a 640×480 Canvas in a Silverlight content region that's sized larger, you will see content that stretches outside those bounds. Ordinarily, you won't see this behavior, because the Silverlight content region is also limited to 640×480 using a style rule, as described earlier, in the section named "The Silverlight Initialization Script."

Positioning Elements in a Canvas

To position an element in the Canvas, you use *attached properties*. Attached properties are another concept that's brought over from WPF. Essentially, an attached property is a property that's defined by one class but used by another. Attached properties are a key extensibility mechanism, because they allow classes to interact in flexible ways even without prior planning. For example, the Canvas defines three attached properties: Left, Top, and ZIndex. Elements inside a Canvas can use these properties to position themselves. This is a better solution than defining these properties as part of some base element classes, because it's more loosely coupled. Elements don't need to be specifically designed to work with the Canvas—they just do. And when Silverlight adds more layout managers, they'll include their own set of layout-related attached properties. It also makes more sense conceptually for the properties to be "attached" to the Canvas, because it's the Canvas that reads these values and acts on them, not the contained element.

To set an attached property in XAML, you use a two-part syntax with a period. The portion on the left is the name of the class where the property is defined (like Canvas), while the portion on the right is the name of the property (like Top). Here's an example that places a Rectangle in a specific location in a Canvas:

```
<Rectangle x:Name="rect" Canvas.Top="30" Canvas.Left="30"
 Fill="Blue" Height="50" Width="50" />
```

Coordinates are measured from the top-left corner, so this creates a shape that's 30 pixels from the top and left edges. If you don't set the Top and Left properties, they default to 0, which places the element in the top-left corner (as was the case with the TextBlock demonstrated in the previous example).

If you want to modify an attached property programmatically, you need to use a slightly more convoluted syntax. The trick is to call the SetValue<T> method on your element. You specify the data type of the property as your type argument, and pass in two parameters: the property you want to modify and the new value you want to set. The following line of code sets the Canvas.Top property that's applied to the Rectangle to 100.

```
rect.SetValue<double>(Canvas.TopProperty, 100);
```

When specifying the property, you use the syntax *ClassName.PropertyName*Property. In other words, the Canvas.Top property is represented by a static field named Canvas.TopProperty.

Layering Elements in a Canvas

If you have more than one overlapping element, you can set the attached Canvas.ZIndex property to control how they are layered.

Ordinarily, all the elements you add have the same ZIndex: 0. When elements have the same ZIndex, they're displayed in the same order that they're declared in the XAML markup. Elements declared later in the markup are displayed on top of elements that are declared earlier.

However, you can promote any element to a higher level by increasing its ZIndex. That's because higher ZIndex elements *always* appear over lower ZIndex elements. Here's an example that uses this technique to reverse the layering of two rectangles:

```
<Rectangle Canvas.Left="60" Canvas.Top="80" Canvas.ZIndex="1"
 Fill="Blue" Width="50" Height="50" />
<Rectangle Canvas.Left="70" Canvas.Top="120" Width="100" Height="50"
 Fill="Yellow" />
```

Now the yellow rectangle will be superimposed over the blue rectangle, despite the fact that it's declared earlier in the markup.

Note The actual values you use for the Canvas.ZIndex property have no meaning. The important detail is how the ZIndex value of one element compares to the ZIndex value of another. You can set the ZIndex using any positive or negative integer.

The ZIndex property is particularly useful if you need to change the position of an element programmatically. Just call the SetValue<T> method on the element you want to modify, with the new ZIndex value you want to apply. Unfortunately, there is no BringToFront() or SendToBack() method—it's up to you to keep track of the highest and lowest ZIndex values if you want to implement this behavior.

Dragging Circles

You can put these concepts together using a simple example.

Figure 6 shows a Silverlight application that allows you to draw and move small circles. Every time you click the Canvas, a red circle appears. To move a circle, you simply click and drag it to a new position. When you click a circle, it changes color from red to green. Finally, when you release your circle, it changes color to orange. There's no limit to how many circles you can add or how many times you can move them around your drawing surface.

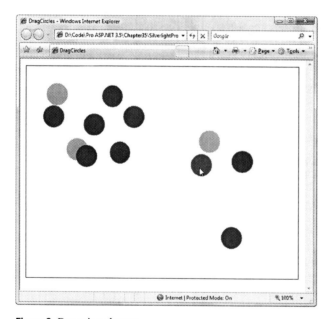

Figure 6. *Dragging shapes*

Each circle is an instance of the Ellipse object. Obviously, you can't define all the ellipses you need in your XAML markup. Instead, you need a way to generate the Ellipse objects dynamically each time the user clicks the Canvas.

Creating an Ellipse object isn't terribly difficult—after all, you can instantiate it like any other .NET object, set its properties, and attach event handlers. You can even use the SetValue<T> method to set attached properties to place it in the correct location in the Canvas. However, there's one more detail to take care of—you need a way to place the Ellipse in the Canvas. This is easy enough, as the

Canvas class exposes a Children collection that holds all the child elements. Once you've added an element to this collection, it will appear in the Canvas.

The XAML page for this example uses a single event handler for the Canvas.MouseLeftButton-Down event. No other elements are defined.

```
<Canvas x:Name="parentCanvas" ...
  MouseLeftButtonDown="canvas_Click">
</Canvas>
```

In the code-behind class, you need two member variables to keep track of whether or not an ellipse-dragging operation is currently taking place:

```
// Keep track of when an ellipse is being dragged.
private bool isDragging = false;

// When an ellipse is clicked, record the exact position
// where the click is made.
private Point mouseOffset;
```

Here's the event-handling code that creates an ellipse when the Canvas is clicked:

```
private void canvas_Click(object o, MouseEventArgs e)
{
    // Create an ellipse (unless the user is in the process
    // of dragging another one).
    if (!isDragging)
    {
        // Give the ellipse a 50-pixel diameter and a red fill.
        Ellipse ellipse = new Ellipse();
        ellipse.Fill = new SolidColorBrush(Colors.Red);
        ellipse.Width = 50;
        ellipse.Height = 50;

        // Use the current mouse position for the center of
        // the ellipse.
        Point point = e.GetPosition(this);
        ellipse.SetValue<double>(Canvas.TopProperty,
        point.Y - ellipse.Height/2);
        ellipse.SetValue<double>(Canvas.LeftProperty,
        point.X - ellipse.Width/2);

        // Watch for left-button clicks.
        ellipse.MouseLeftButtonDown += ellipse_MouseDown;

        // Add the ellipse to the Canvas.
        this.Children.Add(ellipse);
    }
}
```

Not only does this code create the ellipse, it also connects an event handler that responds when the ellipse is clicked. This event handler changes the ellipse color and initiates the ellipse-dragging operation:

```
private void ellipse_MouseDown(object o, MouseEventArgs e)
{
    // Dragging mode begins.
```

```
    isDragging = true;
    Ellipse ellipse = (Ellipse)o;

    // Get the position of the click relative to the ellipse
    // so the top-left corner of the ellipse is (0,0).
    mouseOffset = e.GetPosition(ellipse);

    // Change the ellipse color.
    ellipse.Fill = new SolidColorBrush(Colors.Green);

    // Watch this ellipse for more mouse events.
    ellipse.MouseMove += ellipse_MouseMove;
    ellipse.MouseLeftButtonUp += ellipse_MouseUp;

    // Capture the mouse. This way you'll keep receiveing
    // the MouseMove event even if the user jerks the mouse
    // off the ellipse.
    ellipse.CaptureMouse();
}
```

The ellipse isn't actually moved until the MouseMove event occurs. At this point, the Canvas.Left and Canvas.Top attached properties are set on the ellipse to move it to its new position. The coordinates are set based on the current position of the mouse, taking into account the point where the user initially clicked. This ellipse then moves seamlessly with the mouse, until the left mouse button is released.

```
private void ellipse_MouseMove(object o, MouseEventArgs e)
{
    if (isDragging)
    {
        Ellipse ellipse = (Ellipse)o;

        // Get the position of the ellipse relative to the Canvas.
        Point point = e.GetPosition(this);

        // Move the ellipse.
        ellipse.SetValue<double>(Canvas.TopProperty, point.Y - mouseOffset.Y);
        ellipse.SetValue<double>(Canvas.LeftProperty, point.X - mouseOffset.X);
    }
}
```

When the left mouse button is released, the code changes the color of the ellipse, releases the mouse capture, and stops listening for the MouseMove and MouseUp events. The user can click the ellipse again to start the whole process over.

```
private void ellipse_MouseUp(object o, EventArgs e)
{
    if (isDragging)
    {
        Ellipse ellipse = (Ellipse)o;

        // Change the ellipse color.
        ellipse.Fill = new SolidColorBrush(Colors.Orange);
```

```
        // Don't watch the mouse events any longer.
        ellipse.MouseMove += ellipse_MouseMove;
        ellipse.MouseLeftButtonUp += ellipse_MouseUp;
        ellipse.ReleaseMouseCapture();

        isDragging = false;
    }
}
```

Text

As you've already learned, you use the TextBlock element to add text to your Silverlight user interface. The TextBlock element includes a few key properties, which are described in Table 2.

Table 2. *TextBlock Properties*

Property	Description
FontFamily	Specifies the name of the font you want to use, such as Times New Roman or Arial. This name should not include any formatting information—in other words, don't use a value like Times New Roman Bold. The default value is Portable User Interface, which is an alias for the Lucida Sans font that's included with Silverlight.
FontSize	Specifies the font size in pixels. The default value is 14.666 pixels, which is exactly 11 points.
FontStyle	Specifies whether the font style is normal or italic. The default value is Normal.
FontWeight	Describes the relative weight of a font. The default value is Normal. The FontWeight enumeration defines all the supported values, such as Thin, Light, Medium, Bold, ExtraBold, Black, and so on.
FontStretch	Describes the degree to which a font form is stretched from its normal aspect ratio, by stretching or compressing the letters horizontally. The default value is Normal. The FontStretch enumeration defines all the supported values, such as UltraCondensed, Condensed, Medium, Expanded, and so on.
TextDecorations	Allows you to apply additional graphical detailing to a font using a value from the TextDecorations namespace. Currently, there are just two choices: Normal (the default) and Underline.
TextWrapping	Allows you to wrap text over multiple lines. You can choose NoWrap (the default), Wrap, or WrapWithOverflow. Both Wrap and WrapWithOverflow enable text wrapping. The difference is that WrapWithOverflow allows a single large word to stretch beyond the bounds of the element if there's no space or hyphen to break on, while Wrap will split the word in this scenario.

Note Ordinarily, you don't need to set the Width and Height of a TextBlock. The TextBlock is automatically set high enough to show a single line of the current font, and wide enough to fit all the supplied text (even if that means the TextBlock stretches beyond the bounds of the Silverlight content region, and so isn't visible). However, if you want to use text wrapping, you must set the width of the TextBlock to limit the length of the line. This causes the text content to flow to subsequent lines, and it causes the height of the TextBlock to increase to fit all the text.

Although you can set any font you want using the FontFamily property, there's no guarantee that the font you want will be available on the client's computer. For consistent results, you should use one of the core fonts included with Silverlight and shown in Figure 7.

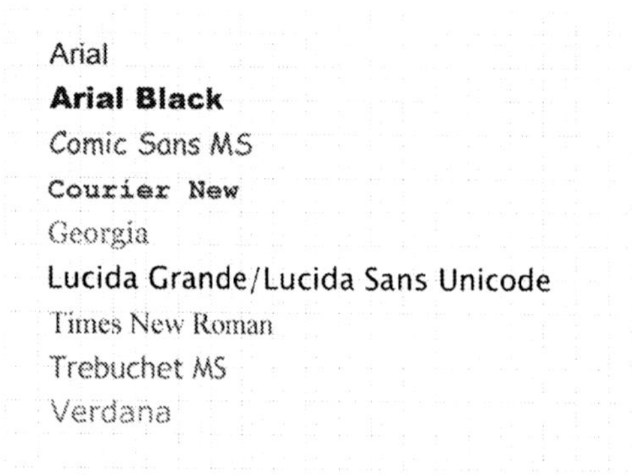

Arial

Arial Black

Comic Sans MS

Courier New

Georgia

Lucida Grande/Lucida Sans Unicode

Times New Roman

Trebuchet MS

Verdana

Figure 7. *Silverlight fonts*

As when setting the fonts for an ASP.NET control, you can supply a comma-separated list that puts the preferred fonts at the beginning and the fallback fonts at the end.

In some situations, you'll want to format just part of the content in a TextBlock. You can do this by nesting a Run element inside a TextBlock. The Run represents any segment of similarly formatted text. Here's an example that uses it:

```
<TextBlock FontFamily="Arial" Width="400" TextWrapping="Wrap">
To create the Silverlight control, you use
the <Run Foreground="Maroon" FontFamily="Courier New">createObjectEx()</Run>
JavaScript function.
</TextBlock>
```

Along with the Run element, you can also place a LineBreak element inside a TextBlock to force a line break.

Note If you place extra whitespace at the beginning or ending of your text inside the <TextBlock>, that whitespace is ignored.

Interacting with HTML

Silverlight includes a set of managed classes that replicate the HTML DOM (document object model) in managed code. These classes allow your Silverlight code to interact with the HTML content on the same page. Depending on the scenario, this interaction might involve reading a control value, updating text, or adding new HTML elements to the page.

The classes you need to perform these feats are part of the System.Silverlight.dll assembly, and they're found in the System.Windows.Browser namespace. These classes include HtmlElement, which represents any HTML element; HtmlObject, which represents a scriptable object that's part of the HTML DOM (for example, a window in a frameset); and HtmlDocument, which represents the complete HTML document. To get access to live instances of these classes, you use the HtmlPage helper class, which provides the static members listed in Table 3.

Table 3. *Static Members of the HtmlPage Class*

Member	Description
BrowserInformation	Returns a BrowserInformation object with information about the browser version, platform, user agent string, and cookie support.
Cookies	Provides a collection of all the current HTTP cookies. You can read or set the values in these cookies. Cookies provide one easy, low-cost way to transfer information from server-side ASP.NET code to client-side Silverlight code.
CurrentBookmark	Returns the optional bookmark portion of the URL string, which can point to a specific anchor on a page. You can use NavigateToBookmark() to move to a different bookmark.
Document	Returns the HtmlDocument object that represents the current HTML document.
DocumentUri	Returns the URL of the current document as a Uri object.
QueryString	Returns the query string portion of the URL as a single long string that you must parse.
Window	Returns an HtmlObject that represents the current browser window.
Navigate()	Sends the browser to another page. You can use an overloaded version of the Navigate() method to specify a target frame.
NavigateToBookmark()	Scrolls to a specific bookmark in the current page.
Submit()	Submits the page. This is useful if you're hosting your Silverlight control in an ASP.NET page, because it triggers a postback that allows server-side code to run.

If you want to interact with the HTML content on the current page, the HtmlPage.Document property is the best starting point. Once you have the HtmlDocument object that represents the page, you can browse down through the element tree (starting at HtmlDocument.DocumentElement) or search for an element with a specific name (using the GetElementByID() or GetElementsByTagName() method of the HtmlDocument class). When you have a specific HtmlElement, you can give it focus, add or remove children, or modify the text content.

Tip You can use the HttpUtility class in the System.Windows.Browser namespace to perform common tasks like HTML encoding and decoding (making text safe for display in a web page) and URL encoding and decoding (making text safe for use in a URL—for example, as a query string argument).

For example, imagine you have this HTML markup just underneath your Silverlight content region (and your Silverlight content region doesn't fill the entire browser window), as shown here:

```
<html xmlns="http://www.w3.org/1999/xhtml">
<head>
    <title>Silverlight Project Test Page </title>
    <script type="text/javascript" src="Silverlight.js"></script>
    <script type="text/javascript" src="TestPage.html.js"></script>
    <style type="text/css">
        .silverlightHost { width: 640px; height: 480px; }
    </style>
```

```
</head>
<body>
    <div id="SilverlightControlHost" class="silverlightHost">
        <script type="text/javascript">
            createSilverlight();
        </script>
    </div>

    <div>
        <hr />
        <p id="paragraph"></p>
    </div>
</body>
</html>
```

You can retrieve an HtmlElement object that represents this paragraph in any Silverlight event handler. The following code retrieves the paragraph and changes the text inside:

```
HtmlElement element = HtmlPage.Document.GetElementByID("paragraph");
element.SetProperty("innerHTML",
  "This HTML paragraph has been updated by Silverlight.");
```

You'll notice that the transition between Silverlight and the HTML DOM isn't quite perfect. Silverlight doesn't include a full HTML DOM, just a lightweight version that standardizes on a basic HtmlElement class. To manipulate this element in a meaningful way, you'll often need to set an HTML DOM property (such as innerHTML in the previous example) using the SetProperty() method and supply the name of the property as a string.

It's possible to interact in the reverse direction—in other words, to allow an HTML element to trigger your Silverlight code in response to a specific event. The easiest way to do so is to use the HtmlElement.AttachEvent() method in your Silverlight code to wire up your event handler. You can do this at any point, although it makes sense to do it once, when your Silverlight content is first initialized, by responding the Canvas.Loaded event.

Here's an example that connects a Silverlight event handler to the onclick event of the HTML <p> element:

```
public partial class Page : Canvas
{
    private void Page_Loaded(object o, EventArgs e)
    {
        InitializeComponent();

        element.AttachEvent("onclick", paragraph_Click);
    }

    private void paragraph_Click(object o, HtmlEventArgs e)
    {
        txt.Text =
      "You clicked an HTML element, but this Silverlight application noticed.";
    }
}
```

Once again, you need to know the name of the HTML DOM event. In other words, you'll need to have your JavaScript skills handy in order to make the leap between Silverlight and HTML.

This technique achieves an impressive feat. Using Silverlight as an intermediary, you can script an HTML page with client-side C# code, instead of using the JavaScript that would normally be required.

Figure 8 shows this code in action.

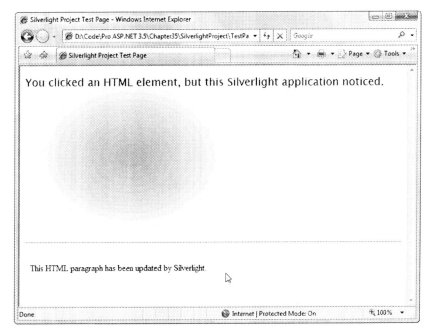

Figure 8. *Silverlight and HTML interaction*

In some cases, you might choose to deepen the integration by another layer. Instead of connecting your Silverlight event handler directly to an HTML DOM event, you might want to connect your event to a JavaScript method, and then have that JavaScript method call into your Silverlight code. This is a bit more involved. In order to make it work, you need to take the following steps:

1. Create a public method in your Silverlight code that exposes the information or functionality you want the web page to use. You'll need to stick to simple data types, like strings, Boolean values, and numbers, unless you want to go through the additional work of serializing your objects to a simpler form.

2. Mark that method with the Scriptable attribute.

3. Mark your Silverlight class (the custom class that derives from Canvas) with the Scriptable attribute.

4. To expose your Silverlight method to JavaScript, call the WebApplication.RegisterScriptable-Object() method in the Page_Loaded() event handler, when your Silverlight content is first loaded.

Provided you take all these steps, your JavaScript code will be able to call your Silverlight method as though it's a method of the Silverlight control.

For example, consider the code-behind class shown here, which includes a scriptable method named RemoveGradient():

```
[Scriptable]
public partial class Page : Canvas
{
    public void Page_Loaded(object o, EventArgs e)
    {
        // Required to initialize variables
        InitializeComponent();

        WebApplication.Current.RegisterScriptableObject("SilverlightPage",
            this);
    }

    [Scriptable]
    public void RemoveGradient()
    {
        this.Background = new SolidColorBrush(Colors.LightGray);
    }

    ...
}
```

The RemoveGradient() method is registered with the name Canvas. As a result, Silverlight will create a property named Canvas, and expose the RemoveGradient() method on that property. You can use any property name you want, but in this example it makes sense to emphasize that the method is attached to the Canvas, because calling it affects the Canvas.

Now all you need is a JavaScript function that calls the RemoveGradient() method:

```
<script type="text/javascript">
  function removeGradient()
  {
      var control = document.getElementById("SilverlightControl");
      control.Content.Canvas.RemoveGradient();
  }
</script>
```

You can trigger this JavaScript method at any time. Here's an example that fires it off when a paragraph is clicked:

```
<p onclick="removeGradient()">Click here to remove the gradient</p>
```

Now clicking the paragraph triggers the removeGradient() JavaScript function, which in turn calls the RemoveGradient() method that's a part of your Silverlight class.

Isolated Storage

Silverlight code isn't permitted to write to arbitrary locations on the file system (or read from them). Obviously, if this ability *were* possible, it would break the web browser's secure sandbox model. However, Silverlight applications that need to store data permanently still have an option. They can use *isolated storage*.

Isolated storage provides a virtual file system that lets you write data to a small, user-specific and application-specific slot of space. The actual location on the hard drive is obfuscated (so there's no way to know exactly where the data will be written beforehand), and the total space available is 512 KB.

A typical location is a path in the form c:\Document and Settings\[UserName]\Local Settings\ Application Data\Isolated Storage\[Guid_Identifier]. Data in one user's isolated store is restricted from all other nonadministrative users.

Note Isolated storage is the .NET equivalent of persistent cookies in an ordinary web page—it allows small bits of information to be stored in a dedicated location that has specific controls in place to prevent malicious attacks (such as code that attempts to fill the hard drive or replace a system file).

Isolated storage is quite easy to use because it exposes the same stream-based model as ordinary file access. You simply use the types in the System.IO.IsolatedStorage namespace. You begin by calling the IsolatedStorageFile.GetUserStoreForApplication() method to get a reference to the isolated store for the current user and application. (Each application gets a separate store.) You can then create a virtual file in that location using the IsolatedStorageFileStream. Here's an example that writes the current date to a virtual file named date.txt in isolated storage. In order to use this code as written, you must import the System.IO and System.IO.IsolatedStorage namespaces.

```
// Write to isolated storage.
try
{
    IsolatedStorageFile store =
        IsolatedStorageFile.GetUserStoreForApplication();

    using (IsolatedStorageFileStream fs = new IsolatedStorageFileStream(
      "date.txt", FileMode.Create, store))
    {
        StreamWriter w = new StreamWriter(fs);
        w.Write(DateTime.Now);
        w.Close();
    }
    txtData.Text = "Data written to date.txt";
}
catch (Exception err)
{
    txtData.Text = err.Message;
}
```

Retrieving information is just as easy. You simply need to open the IoslatedStorageFileStream in read mode:

```
// Read from isolated storage.
try
{
    IsolatedStorageFile store =
        IsolatedStorageFile.GetUserStoreForApplication();

    using (IsolatedStorageFileStream fs = new IsolatedStorageFileStream(
      "date.txt", FileMode.Open, store))
    {
        StreamReader r = new StreamReader(fs);
        txtData.Text = r.ReadLine();
        r.Close();
    }
}
```

```
catch (Exception err)
{
    // An exception will occur if you attempt to open a file that doesn't exist.
    txtData.Text = err.Message;
}
```

You can try this code out with the IsolatedStorageTest.html page included with the downloadable examples.

Unlike the full .NET Framework, the Silverlight version of the IsolatedStorageFile class doesn't include methods like IsolatedStorageFile.GetFileNames() and IsolatedStorageFile.GetDirectoryNames(), which allow you to enumerate the contents of the isolated store. Instead, you're limited to getting the current store for the current application and creating or retrieving a file by name.

Silverlight and ASP.NET

The Silverlight examples you've seen so far can be used in a basic, stand-alone website or in an ASP.NET web application. If you want to use them in an ASP.NET website, you simply need to add the Silverlight files to your website folder or web project. You copy the same files that you copy when deploying a Silverlight application—everything except the source code files. (For more information about Silverlight deployment, refer to the "Silverlight Compilation" section .)

Unfortunately, the ASP.NET development process and the Silverlight development process aren't yet integrated in Visual Studio. As a result, you'll need to compile your Silverlight project separately and copy the compiled assembly by hand. (You can't simply add a reference to the compiled assembly, because Visual Studio will place the referenced assembly in the Bin folder, so it's accessible to your ASP.NET server-side code, which isn't what you want. Instead, you need to place it in the ClientBin folder, which is where your HTML entry page expects to find it.)

This approach allows you to place Silverlight and ASP.NET pages side by side on the same website; but they aren't in any way integrated. You can navigate from one page to another (for example, use a link to send a user from an ASP.NET web form to a Silverlight entry page), but there's no interaction between the server-side and client-side code. In many situations, this design is completely reasonable, because the Silverlight application represents a distinct "applet" that's available in your website. In other scenarios, you might want to share part of your data model, or integrate server-side processing and client-side processing as part of a single task.

ASP.NET Futures

The ASP.NET Futures release includes two ASP.NET web controls that render Silverlight content: Xaml and Media (which are described in the following sections). Both of these controls are placed in an assembly named Microsoft.Web.Preview.dll, which you can find in a directory with a name like c:\Program Files\Microsoft ASP.NET\ASP.NET Futures July 2007\v1.2.61025\3.5.

In order to use the Xaml and Media controls, you need a reference to the Microsoft.Web.Preview.dll assembly. You also need to register a control tag prefix for the Microsoft.Web.Preview.UI.Controls namespace (which is where the Xaml control is located). Here's the Register directive that you can add to a web page (just after the Page directive) to use the familiar asp tag prefix with the new ASP.NET Futures controls:

```
<%@ Register Assembly="Microsoft.Web.Preview"
 Namespace="Microsoft.Web.Preview.UI.Controls" TagPrefix="asp" %>
```

Alternatively, you can register the control prefix in your web.config file so that it automatically applies to all pages:

```
<?xml version="1.0"?>
<configuration>
  ...
  <system.web>
    <pages>
      <controls>
        <add tagPrefix="asp" namespace="Microsoft.Web.Preview.UI.Controls"
         assembly="Microsoft.Web.Preview" />
        ...
      </controls>
    </pages>
    ...
  </system.web>
  ...
</configuration>
```

Rather than adding the assembly reference and editing the web.config file by hand, you can use a Visual Studio website template. Choose File ➤ New ➤ Web Site and select ASP.NET Futures Web Site. When you take this approach, you'll end up with many more new settings in the web.config file, which are added to enable other ASP.NET Futures features that aren't related to Silverlight. Once you've finished these configuration steps, you're ready to place the Xaml and Media controls in a web page. You'll need to type the markup for these controls by hand, as they won't appear in the Toolbox. (You could add them to the Toolbox, but it's probably not worth the effort considering that there are likely to be newer builds of ASP.NET Futures in the near future.)

The Xaml Control

As you learned earlier, the HTML entry page creates a Silverlight content region using a <div> place-holder and a small snippet of JavaScript code. There's no reason you can't duplicate the same approach to place a Silverlight content region in an ASP.NET web form. However, there's a shortcut that you can use. Rather than creating the <div> tag and adding the JavaScript code by hand, you can use the Xaml control.

The Xaml control uses essentially the same technique as the HTML entry page you saw earlier, rendering a <div> tag and adding the JavaScript. The advantage is that you specify the XAML page you want to use (and configure a few additional details) using properties on the server side. That gives you a slightly simpler model to work with, and an easy way to vary these details dynamically (for example, choose a different XAML page based on server-side information, like the identity of the current user).

Here's the ASP.NET markup you'd use to show a XAML file named Page.xaml:

```
<form id="form1" runat="server">
  <asp:ScriptManager ID="ScriptManager1" runat="server" />
  <asp:Xaml XamlUrl="~/Page.xaml" runat="server"></asp:Xaml>
</form>
```

You can set a number of properties on the Xaml control to configure how the Silverlight content region will be created, including Height, Width, MinimumSilverlightVersion, SilverlightBackColor, and EnableHtmlAccess. You can also attach the Xaml control to two JavaScript functions. Set OnClientXamlError with the name of a JavaScript function that will be triggered if the Silverlight XAML can't be loaded, and set OnClientXamlLoaded with the name of the JavaScript function that will be triggered if the Silverlight content region is created successfully.

You also need to add the XAML page to your website. Unfortunately, the current build of ASP.NET Futures doesn't include a XAML template for Silverlight 1.1 content. Instead, it includes a XAML template for Silverlight 1.0 content, complete with a JavaScript code-behind file. (This choice was made for compatibility with Silverlight 1.0, which doesn't support client-side C# and the scaled-down CLR.)

The easiest way to use Silverlight 1.1 content with the Xaml control is to create your XAML pages in a dedicated Silverlight project. You can then copy the XAML files and the ClientBin folder to your ASP.NET website. This extra work isn't the result of a technical limitation—it's simply a limitation of pre-release software.

The Media Control

The Media web control gives you a server-side abstraction over the MediaElement class from Silverlight. (As explained earlier, the MediaElement is a Silverlight element that manages the playback of an audio or video file.)

The obvious question is, "When should you use the MediaElement, and when should you prefer the server-side Media web control?" They both amount to the same thing—after all, the server-side Media web control renders a MediaElement, although it requires slightly more work on the server to do so. The primary advantage to using the Media web control is that you have the chance to set some of its properties using server-side code. For example, you could set the media URL based on information from a database and even extract it through data binding.

Here's an example of how you might define the Media control:

```
<asp:Media runat="server" ID="Media1"
  AutoPlay="true" MediaUrl="MyVideoFile.wmv"
  SilverlightBackColor="blue" MediaSkin="Professional"
  Height="240" Width="320" />
```

This creates a Silverlight control with a media player in it, as shown in Figure 9.

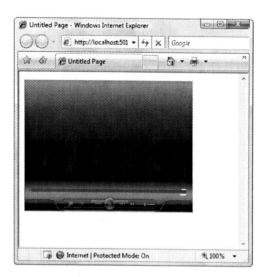

Figure 9. *The Silverlight media player*

The media player attempts to access the MyViewFile.wmv file, and begins playing it immediately. In order to streamline the video playback experience, the media player downloads and buffers small chunks of video data as it plays. Best of all, the Silverlight media player works without requiring

Windows Media Player. It's more lightweight and performant, and the user interface (playback buttons, skin, and so on) is more customizable.

To get the most out of Silverlight's media playing ability, you need to take a closer look at the properties provided by the Media control. Table 4 lists some of the most important.

Table 4. *Properties of the Media Web Control*

Property	Description
MediaUrl	Identifies the location of the media file. You can use .wma, .wmv, .mp3 and .asx file types. You can specify a relative path for a file on your web server (as in the previous example), or you can supply a full URL that points to another location.
AutoPlay	Sets whether playback starts immediately when the page is initialized. The default is false, which means the user will need to use the playback controls to initiate playback.
AutoScale	Sets whether the XAML should be resized to fit the player size. The default is true.
LoopCount	Sets the number of times to loop (repeat) the media file. Use a value of 0 to loop the media file continuously.
MediaSkin	Specifies the "skin" that determines the appearance of the media player. The media player includes several built-in skins that include different graphics, colors, and animated effects. Each skin is defined in a XAML resource that's embedded in the Silverlight assemblies. Skins are defined by the MediaSkin enumeration and include AudioGray, Basic, Blitz, Classic, Expression, Game, Professional, and Simple.
PlaceholderImageUrl	Specifies a URL to a placeholder image that will be shown while the media file is being opened. Once the media file is opened, this image is replaced with the first frame of your video.
Volume	Sets the volume as a value between 0 (silent) and 1 (the maximum volume).
Muted	Determines whether the audio should be muted initially. The default is false.
StartTime	Specifies a location in the media file (as an offset in seconds) where playback should start. By default, playback starts at the beginning of the file.
Duration	Sets the number of seconds that media should play before stopping. By default, the entire media file is played.

There are several more features of the Media control that aren't covered here:

- You can define chapters that link to specific locations in your media file, and show them in the media player. The user can then jump directly to one of these chapters.

- You can export any of the media player's skins as XAML, customize it, and then use that customized version on your web page.

- You can use JavaScript methods to control media playback. This gives you another way to interact with ASP.NET, as you can create ASP.NET AJAX routines that interact with the media player. You can also set various On*Xxx* properties (like OnClientMediaEnded and OnClientMedia- Failed) to trigger a JavaScript function when a specific event happens in the media player.

For information about these more advanced tasks, refer to http://quickstarts.asp.net/Futures/Silverlight/media.aspx.

Communicating Between Silverlight and ASP.NET

If your website includes ASP.NET code and Silverlight content, you may want to pass some information from one side to another. There are several ways that you can allow this sort of interaction. Here are two simple approaches:

- When you redirect the user from an ASP.NET web page to a Silverlight entry page, you can supply startup information in a cookie or a query string. The Silverlight code can access this information using the classes in the System.Windows.Browser namespace, as described in the "Interacting with HTML."

- Similarly, your Silverlight application can use the query string or set a cookie before navigating to an ASP.NET web form by calling HtmlPage.Navigate(). If the Silverlight control is on an ASP.NET web form, it can call HtmlPage.Submit() to trigger a postback. This is also described in the "Interacting with HTML" section.

Both of these techniques allow you to send information as you switch from the client side to the server side, and vice versa. For example, if your Silverlight control calls HtmlPage.Submit(), the entire page is posted back, the Silverlight application ends, and the ASP.NET objects are created. If you want the user to perform another action with your Silverlight application, you need to return a new page with the Silverlight content. Then, the Silverlight control needs to be created and initialized all over again.

Another option is to allow a long-running Silverlight application to trigger some server-side code without actually posting back the page. That way, the application continues running. The easiest way to do this is to have your Silverlight application call an ASP.NET web service, just as you would with an ASP.NET AJAX page. The development model is quite convenient—when you add a web reference to your web service in the Silverlight project, Visual Studio generates the proxy class you need to call the web service. You simply need to instantiate the proxy class and call its methods, just as you would in a full-fledged .NET application that calls a web service. (For more information about designing web services, generating proxy classes in Visual Studio, and calling them in rich clients, you can refer to Bonus Chapter 2, Bonus Chapter 3, and Bonus Chapter 4, which are provided on at (http://www.apress.com/book/view/1590598938).

Note In the current Silverlight build, you can't launch cross-domain web service calls. In other words, you can only make a call to the website where the Silverlight page is located.

Drawing in 2D

As you've probably noticed, Silverlight includes relatively few elements, and none of the higher-level controls that rich client developers are used to (like buttons, text boxes, list boxes, scroll bars, and so on). All of these details are planned for future editions, but the first versions of Silverlight concentrate on two different areas—2D drawing and animation. Coming up, you'll consider these two feature areas.

Silverlight's 2D drawing support is the basic foundation for many more sophisticated features, such as custom-drawn controls, interactive graphics, and animation. Even if you plan to code at a higher level and deal with more capable Silverlight controls (when they appear), you'll need to have a solid understanding of drawing fundamentals such as geometries, brushes, and transparency.

CREATING XAML GRAPHICS

In many cases, you won't create Silverlight art by hand. Instead, you (or a designer) will use a design tool to create vector art, and then export it to XAML. The exported XAML document you'll end up with is essentially a Canvas that contains a combination of Shape elements. You can place that Canvas inside an existing Canvas to show your artwork.

Microsoft Expression Design is one example of a design tool that supports XAML natively. However, plug-ins and conversion tools are available for many other popular formats. For example, you can convert an Adobe Illustrator document to XAML using the converter at `http://www.mikeswanson.com/xamlexport`.

Silverlight supports a surprisingly large subset of the drawing features from WPF, its more capable sibling. In this section, you'll consider how you can create complex geometries complete with arcs and curves, how you can great gradients and other effects with brushes, and how you can use partial transparency. But every Silverlight drawing begins with a relatively simple ingredient—shapes.

Simple Shapes

Silverlight includes a small set of elements that represent shapes: the Rectangle, Ellipse, Line, Polyline, Polygon, and Path. You've already encountered the Rectangle and Ellipse, but you haven't considered all the details that they entail. For example, you've focused on using the Fill property to paint the inside of your rectangles and ellipses, without considering the Stroke property that lets you drawn an outline around it.

All the shape classes share some common functionality that's based on the properties listed in Table 5. In the following sections, you'll start by taking a closer look at the shape classes.

Table 5. *Shape Properties*

Name	Description
Fill	Sets the brush object that paints the surface of the shape (everything inside its borders).
Stroke	Sets the brush object that paints the edge of the shape (its border).
StrokeThickness	Sets the thickness of the border, in pixels. When drawing a line, Silverlight splits the width on each side. So a line that's 10 units wide gets 5 units of space on each side of where a single-unit line would be drawn.
StrokeStartLineCap and StrokeEndLineCap	Determine the contour of the edge of the beginning and end of the line. These properties only have an effect for the Line, the Polyline, and (sometimes) the Path shapes. All other shapes are closed, and so have no starting and ending point.
StrokeDashArray, StrokeDashOffset, and StrokeDashCap	Allow you to create a dashed border around a shape. You can control the size and frequency of the dashes and how the edge where each dash line begins and ends is contoured.
StrokeLineJoin and StrokeMiterLimit	Determine the contour of the corners of a shape. Technically, these properties affect the *vertices* where different lines meet, such as the corners of a Rectangle. These properties have no effect for shapes without corners, such as Line and Ellipse.

Note Remember, the Silverlight shape classes are genuine elements. That means they support all the standard element events, allowing you to react to mouse movement and mouse clicks to create an interactive interface.

Rectangle and Ellipse

The Rectangle and Ellipse are the two simplest shapes. To create either one, set the familiar Height and Width properties (inherited from FrameworkElement) to define the size of your shape, and then set the Fill or Stroke property (or both) to make the shape visible.

The Ellipse class doesn't add any properties to those inherited from FrameworkElement. The Rectangle class adds just two: RadiusX and RadiusY. When set to nonzero values, these properties allow you to create nicely rounded corners.

You can think of RadiusX and RadiusY as describing an ellipse that's used just to fill in the corners of the rectangle. For example, if you set both properties to 10, Silverlight draws your corners using the edge of a circle that has a radius of 10 pixels. As you make your radius larger, more of your rectangle will be rounded off. If you increase RadiusY more than RadiusX, your corners will round off more gradually along the left and right sides and more sharply along the top and bottom edge. If you increase the RadiusX property to match your rectangle's width and increase RadiusY to match its height, you'll end up converting your rectangle into an ordinary ellipse.

Figure 10 shows a few rectangles with rounded corners.

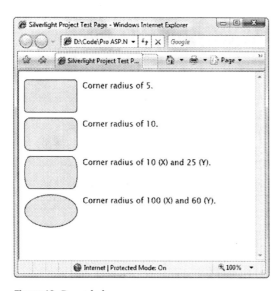

Figure 10. *Rounded corners*

Line

The Line shape represents a straight line that connects one point to another. The starting and ending points are set by four properties: X1 and Y1 (for the first point) and X2 and Y2 (for the second). For example, here's a line that stretches from (0, 0) to (10, 100):

```
<Line Stroke="Blue" X1="0" Y1="0" X2="10" Y2="100"></Line>
```

The Fill property has no effect for a line. You must set the Stroke property.

The coordinates you use in a line are relative to the top-left corner where the line is placed. When you place a line at a specific position in a Canvas, the starting point of the line is offset by the Canvas coordinates. Consider this line:

```
<Line Stroke="Blue" X1="0" Y1="0" X2="10" Y2="100"
 Canvas.Left="5" Canvas.Top="100"></Line>
```

It stretches from (0, 0) to (10, 100), using a coordinate system that treats the point (5, 100) on the Canvas as (0, 0). That makes it equivalent to this line that doesn't use the Top and Left properties:

```
<Line Stroke="Blue" X1="5" Y1="100" X2="15" Y2="200"></Line>
```

It's up to you whether you use the position properties when you place a Line on a Canvas. Often, you can simplify your line drawing by picking a good starting point.

Polyline

The Polyline class allows you to draw a sequence of connected straight lines. You simply supply a list of X and Y coordinates using the Points property. Technically, the Points property requires a Point-Collection object, but you fill this collection in XAML using a lean string-based syntax. You simply need to supply a list of points and add a space or comma between each coordinate.

A Polyline can have as few as two points. For example, here's a Polyline that duplicates the line in the previous example, which stretches from (5, 100) to (15, 200):

```
<Polyline Stroke="Blue" Points="5,100 15,200"></Polyline>
```

And here's a more complex PolyLine that begins at (10, 150). The points move steadily to the right, oscillating between higher and lower Y values:

```
<Polyline Stroke="Blue" StrokeThickness="5"
 Points="10,150 30,140 50,160 70,130 90,170 110,120
 130,180 150,110 170,190 190,100 210,240" >
</Polyline>
```

Figure 11 shows the final line.

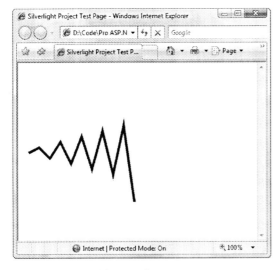

Figure 11. *A line with several segments*

Polygon

The Polygon is virtually the same as the Polyline. Like the Polyline class, the Polygon class has a Points collection that takes a list of coordinates. The only difference is that the Polygon adds a final line segment that connects the final point to the starting point. (If your final point is already the same as the first point, the Polygon class has no difference.) You can fill the interior of this shape using the Fill brush.

In a simple shape where the lines never cross, it's easy to fill the interior. However, sometimes you'll have a more complex Polygon where it's not necessarily obvious what portions are "inside" the shape (and should be filled) and what portions are outside.

For example, consider Figure 12, which features a line that crosses more than one other line, leaving an irregular region at the center that you may or may not want to fill. Obviously, you can control exactly what gets filled by breaking this drawing down into smaller shapes. But you may not need to.

Every Polygon and Polyline includes a FillRule property that lets you choose between two different approaches for filling in regions. Understanding how FillRule works is the key to filling in the regions you want in a compound shape.

By default, Fill Rule is set to EvenOdd. In order to decide whether to fill a region, Silverlight counts the number of lines that must be crossed to reach the outside of the shape. If this number is odd, the region is filled in; if it's even, the region isn't filled. In the center area of Figure 12, you must cross two lines to get out of the shape, so it's not filled.

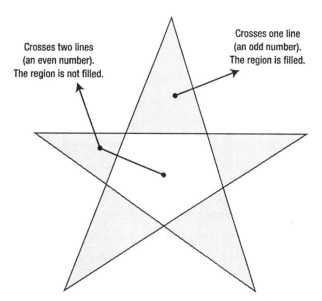

Figure 12. *Determining fill areas when FillRule is EvenOdd*

Silverlight also includes a Nonzero fill rule, which is a little trickier. Essentially, with Nonzero, Silverlight follows the same line-counting process as EvenOdd, but it takes into account the *direction* that each line flows. If the number of lines going in one direction (say, left to right) is equal to the number going in the opposite direction (right to left), the region is not filled. If the difference between these two counts is not zero, the region *is* filled. In the shape from the previous example, the interior region is filled if you set FillRule to Nonzero. Figure 13 shows why. (In this example, the points are numbered in the order they are drawn, and arrows show the direction in which each line is drawn.)

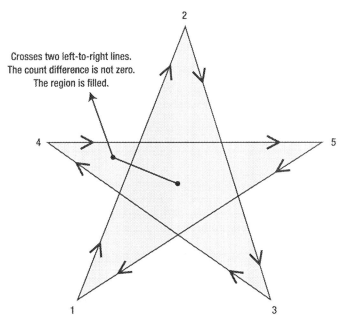

Figure 13. *Determining fill areas when FillRule is Nonzero*

Note If there is an odd number of lines, the difference between the two counts can't be zero. Thus, the Nonzero fill rule always fills at least as much as the EvenOdd rule, plus possibly a bit more.

The tricky part about Nonzero is that its fill settings depend on *how* you draw the shape, not what the shape itself looks like. For example, you could draw the same shape in such a way that the center isn't filled (although it's much more awkward—you'd begin by drawing the inner region and then draw the outside spikes in the reverse direction).

Here's the markup that draws the star shown in Figure 13:

```
<Polygon Stroke="Blue" StrokeThickness="1" Fill="Yellow"
 Canvas.Left="10" Canvas.Top="175" FillRule="Nonzero"
 Points="15,200 68,70 110,200 0,125 134,125">
</Polygon>
```

Paths and Geometries

The Path is a shape with a difference. Unlike the simple shapes you've considered so far, the Path has the ability to encompass any simple shape, groups of shapes, and more complex ingredients such as curves.

The Path class includes a single property, named Data, that accepts a Geometry object that defines the shape (or shapes) the path includes. You can't create a Geometry object directly because it's an abstract class. Instead, you need to use one of the derived classes listed in Table 6.

Table 6. *Geometry Classes*

Name	Description
LineGeometry	Represents a straight line, which is the geometry equivalent of the Line shape
RectangleGeometry	Represents a rectangle (optionally with rounded corners), which is the geometry equivalent of the Rectangle shape
EllipseGeometry	Represents an ellipse, which is the geometry equivalent of the Ellipse shape
GeometryGroup	Adds any number of Geometry objects to a single Path, using the Even-Odd or Nonzero fill rule to determine what regions to fill
PathGeometry	Represents a more complex figure that's composed of arcs, curves, and lines, and can be open or closed

At this point, you might be wondering what the difference is between a path and a geometry. A geometry *defines* a shape. A path allows you to *draw* the shape. Thus, the Geometry object defines details such as the coordinates and size of your shape, while the Path object supplies the Stroke and Fill brushes you'll use to paint it. The Path class also includes element features such as mouse and keyboard handling.

In the following sections, you'll take a quick look at the classes that derive from Geometry.

Note Geometries aren't just for use with the Path. You can also use them with *clipping* to define a shaped region that bounds an element. To use clipping, simply set the Clip property of the element. For example, if you set the Clip property of a Canvas to an ellipse, all the content that would ordinarily be drawn outside that ellipse won't be displayed.

Line, Rectangle, and Ellipse Geometries

The LineGeometry, RectangleGeometry, and EllipseGeometry classes map directly to the Line, Rectangle, and Ellipse shapes. For example, you can convert this markup that uses the Rectangle element:

```
<Rectangle Fill="Yellow" Stroke="Blue"
  Width="100" Height="50"></Rectangle>
```

to this markup that uses the Path element:

```
<Path Fill="Yellow" Stroke="Blue">
  <Path.Data>
    <RectangleGeometry Rect="0,0 100,50"></RectangleGeometry>
  </Path.Data>
</Path>
```

The only real difference is that the Rectangle shape takes Height and Width values, while the RectangleGeometry takes four numbers that describe the size *and* location of the rectangle. The first two numbers describe the X, Y coordinate point where the top-left corner will be placed, while the last two numbers set the width and height of the rectangle. You can start the rectangle out at (0, 0) to get the same effect as an ordinary Rectangle element, or you can offset the rectangle using different values. The RectangleGeometry class also includes the RadiusX and RadiusY properties that let you round the corners (as described earlier).

Similarly, you can convert the following Line:

```
<Line Stroke="Blue" X1="0" Y1="0" X2="10" Y2="100"></Line>
```

to this LineGeometry:

```
<Path Fill="Yellow" Stroke="Blue">
  <Path.Data>
    <LineGeometry StartPoint="0,0" EndPoint="10,100"></LineGeometry>
  </Path.Data>
</Path>
```

And you can convert an Ellipse like this:

```
<Ellipse Fill="Yellow" Stroke="Blue"
  Width="100" Height="50"></Ellipse>
```

to this EllipseGeometry:

```
<Path Fill="Yellow" Stroke="Blue">
  <Path.Data>
    <EllipseGeometry RadiusX="50" RadiusY="25" Center="50,25"></EllipseGeometry>
  </Path.Data>
</Path>
```

Notice that the two radius values are simply half of the width and height values. You can also use the Center property to offset the location of the ellipse. In this example, the center is placed in the exact middle of the ellipse bounding box, so that it's drawn in exactly the same way as the Ellipse shape.

Overall, these simple geometries work in exactly the same way as the corresponding shapes. You get the added ability to offset rectangles and ellipses, but that's not necessary if you're placing your shapes on a Canvas, which already gives you the ability to position your shapes at a specific position. In fact, if this were all you could do with geometries, you probably wouldn't bother to use the Path element. The difference appears when you decide to combine more than one geometry in the same path, as described in the next section.

Combining Shapes with GeometryGroup

The simplest way to combine geometries is to use the GeometryGroup class and nest the other Geometry-derived objects inside. Here's an example that places an ellipse next to a square:

```
<Path Fill="Yellow" Stroke="Blue" Canvas.Top="10" Canvas.Left="10" >
  <Path.Data>
    <GeometryGroup>
      <RectangleGeometry Rect="0,0 100,100" />
      <EllipseGeometry Center="150,50" RadiusX="35" RadiusY="25"/>
    </GeometryGroup>
  </Path.Data>
</Path>
```

The effect of this markup is the same as if you supplied two Path elements, one with the Rectangle-Geometry and one with the EllipseGeometry (and that's the same as if you used a Rectangle and Ellipse shape instead). However, there's one advantage to this approach. You've replaced two elements with one, which means you've reduced the overhead of your user interface.

There's also a drawback to combining geometries in a single Path element—namely, you won't be able to perform event handling of the different shapes separately. Instead, the Path element will fire all mouse events. However, you can still manipulate the nested RectangleGeometry and Ellipse-Geometry objects independently to change the overall path. For example, each geometry provides a Transform property that you can set to stretch, skew, or rotate that part of the path.

The GeometryGroup becomes more interesting when your shapes intersect. Rather than simply treating your drawing as a combination of solid shapes, the GeometryGroup uses its FillRule property (which can be EvenOdd or Nonzero, as described earlier to decide what shapes to fill. Consider what happens if you alter the markup shown earlier like this, placing the ellipse over the square:

```
<Path Fill="Yellow" Stroke="Blue" Canvas.Top="10" Canvas.Left="10" >
  <Path.Data>
    <GeometryGroup>
      <RectangleGeometry Rect="0,0 100,100"/>
      <EllipseGeometry Center="50,50" RadiusX="35" RadiusY="25"/>
    </GeometryGroup>
  </Path.Data>
</Path>
```

Now this markup creates a square with an ellipse-shaped hole in it (through which you can see any content that's layered underneath). If you change FillRule to Nonzero, you'll get a solid ellipse over a solid rectangle, both with the same yellow fill.

Curves and Lines with PathGeometry

PathGeometry is the superpower of geometries. It can draw anything that the other geometries can, and much more. The only drawback is a lengthier (and somewhat more complex) syntax.

Every PathGeometry object is built out of one or more PathFigure objects (which are stored in the PathGeometry.Figures collection). Each PathFigure is a continuous set of connected lines and curves that can be closed or open. The figure is closed if the end of the last line in the figure connects to the beginning of the first line.

The PathFigure class has four key properties, as described in Table 7.

Table 7. *PathFigure Properties*

Name	Description
StartPoint	This is a Point that indicates where the line for the figure begins.
Segments	This is a collection of PathSegment objects that are used to draw the figure.
IsClosed	If true, Silverlight adds a straight line to connect the starting and ending points (if they aren't the same).
IsFilled	If true, the area inside the figure is filled in using the Path.Fill brush.

So far, this all sounds fairly straightforward. The PathFigure is a shape that's drawn using an unbroken line that consists of a number of segments. However, the trick is that there are several type of segments, all of which derive from the PathSegment class. Some are simple, like the LineSegment that draws a straight line. Others, like the BezierSegment, draw curves and are correspondingly more complex. Overall, when using a PathGeometry, your markup will take this form:

```
<Path Stroke="Blue">
  <Path.Data>
    <PathGeometry>
      <PathFigure>
        <segment/>
        <segment/>
        ...
      </PathFigure>
    </PathGeometry>
```

```
    </Path.Data>
</Path>
```

You can mix and match different segments freely to build your figure. Table 8 lists the segment classes you can use.

Table 8. *PathSegment Classes*

Name	Description
LineSegment	Creates a straight line between two points.
ArcSegment	Creates an elliptical arc between two points.
BezierSegment	Creates a Bézier curve between two points.
QuadraticBezierSegment	Creates a simpler form of Bézier curve that has one control point instead of two, and is faster to calculate.
PolyLineSegment	Creates a series of straight lines. You can get the same effect using multiple LineSegment objects, but a single PolyLine-Segment is more concise.
PolyBezierSegment	Creates a series of Bézier curves.
PolyQuadraticBezierSegment	Creates a series of simpler quadratic Bézier curves.

In the following sections, you'll see several examples of Path objects that use these segments to create basic shapes.

Straight Lines

It's easy enough to create simple lines using the LineSegment and PathGeometry classes. You simply set the StartPoint and add one LineSegment for each section of the line. The LineSegment.Point property identifies the endpoint of each segment.

For example, the following markup begins at (10, 100), draws a straight line to (100, 100), and then draws a line from that point to (100, 50). Because the PathFigure.IsClosed property is set to true, a final line segment is adding connection (100, 50) to (0, 0). The final result is a right-angled triangle:

```
<Path Stroke="Blue">
  <Path.Data>
    <PathGeometry>
      <PathFigure IsClosed="True" StartPoint="10,100">
        <LineSegment Point="100,100" />
        <LineSegment Point="100,50" />
      </PathFigure>
    </PathGeometry>
  </Path.Data>
</Path>
```

Arcs

Arcs are a little more interesting than straight lines. You identify the endpoint of the line using the ArcSegment.Point property, just as you would with a LineSegment. However, the PathFigure draws a curved line from the starting point (or the endpoint of the previous segment) to the endpoint of your arc. This curved connecting line is actually a portion of the edge of an ellipse.

Obviously, the endpoint isn't enough information to draw the arc because there are many curves (some gentle, some more extreme) that could connect two points. You also need to indicate the size of the imaginary ellipse that's being used to draw the arc. You do this using the ArcSegment.Size property, which supplies the X radius and the Y radius of the ellipse. The larger the size of the imaginary ellipse, the more gradually its edge curves.

░**Note**　For any two points, there is a practical maximum and minimum size for the ellipse. The maximum occurs when you create an ellipse so large that the line segment you're drawing appears straight. Increasing the size beyond this point has no effect. The minimum occurs when the ellipse is small enough that a full semicircle connects the two points. Shrinking the size beyond this point also has no effect.

Here's an example that creates the gentle arc shown in Figure 14:

```
<Path Stroke="Blue" StrokeThickness="3">
  <Path.Data>
    <PathGeometry>
      <PathFigure IsClosed="False" StartPoint="10,100" >
        <ArcSegment Point="250,150" Size="200,300" />
      </PathFigure>
    </PathGeometry>
  </Path.Data>
</Path>
```

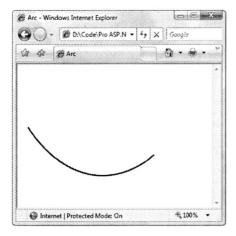

Figure 14. *A simple arc*

So far, arcs sound fairly straightforward. However, it turns out that even with the start and endpoint and the size of the ellipse, you still don't have all the information you need to draw your arc unambiguously. In the previous example, you're relying on two default values that may not be set to your liking.

To understand the problem, you need to consider the other ways that an arc can connect the same two points. If you picture two points on an ellipse, it's clear that you can connect them in two ways—by going around the short side, or by going around the long side. Figure 15 illustrates.

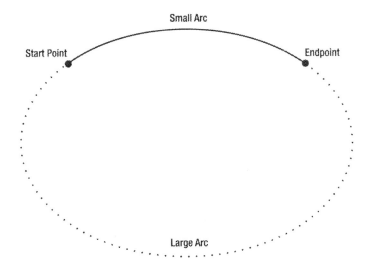

Figure 15. *Two ways to trace a curve along an ellipse*

You set the direction using the ArcSegment.IsLargeArc property, which can be true or false. The default value is false, which means you get the shorter of the two arcs.

Even once you've set the direction, there is still one point of ambiguity—where the ellipse is placed. For example, imagine you draw an arc that connects a point on the left with a point on the right, using the shortest possible arc. The curve that connects these two points could be stretched down and then up or it could be flipped so that it curves up and then down. The arc you get depends on the order in which you define the two points in the arc and the ArcSegment.SweepDirection property, which can be Counterclockwise (the default) or Clockwise. Figure 16 shows the difference.

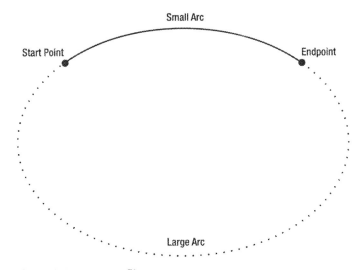

Figure 16. *Two ways to flip a curve*

Bézier Curves

Bézier curves connect two line segments using a complex mathematical formula that incorporates two *control points* that determine how the curve is shaped. Bézier curves are an ingredient in virtually every vector drawing application ever created because they're remarkably flexible. Using nothing more than a start point, an endpoint, and two control points, you can create a surprisingly wide variety of smooth curves (including loops). Figure 17 shows a classic Bézier curve. Two small circles indicate the control points, and a dashed line connects each control point to the end of the line it affects the most.

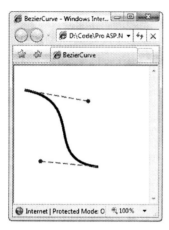

Figure 17. *A Bézier curve*

Even without understanding the math underpinnings, it's fairly easy to get the "feel" of how Bézier curves work. Essentially, the two control points do all the magic. They influence the curve in two ways:

- At the starting point, a Bézier curve runs parallel with the line that connects it to the first control point. At the ending point, the curve runs parallel with the line that connects it to the endpoint. (In between, it curves.)

- The degree of curvature is determined by the distance to the two control points. If one control point is farther away, it exerts a stronger "pull."

To define a Bézier curve in markup, you supply three points. The first two points (BezierSegment.Point1 and BezierSegment.Point2) are the control points. The third point (BezierSegment.Point3) is the endpoint of the curve. As always, the starting point is that starting point of the path or wherever the previous segment left off.

The example shown in Figure 17 includes three separate components, each of which uses a different stroke and thus requires a separate Path element. The first path creates the curve, the second adds the dashed lines, and the third applies the circles that indicate the control points. Here's the complete markup:

```
<Canvas ...>
  <Path Stroke="Blue" StrokeThickness="5" Canvas.Top="20">
    <Path.Data>
      <PathGeometry>
        <PathFigure StartPoint="10,10">
          <BezierSegment Point1="130,30" Point2="40,140"
```

```
            Point3="150,150"></BezierSegment>
        </PathFigure>
      </PathGeometry>
    </Path.Data>
  </Path>
  <Path Stroke="Green" StrokeThickness="2" StrokeDashArray="5 2" Canvas.Top="20">
    <Path.Data>
      <GeometryGroup>
        <LineGeometry StartPoint="10,10" EndPoint="130,30"></LineGeometry>
        <LineGeometry StartPoint="40,140" EndPoint="150,150"></LineGeometry>
      </GeometryGroup>
    </Path.Data>
  </Path>
  <Path Fill="Red" Stroke="Red" StrokeThickness="8"  Canvas.Top="20">
    <Path.Data>
      <GeometryGroup>
        <EllipseGeometry Center="130,30"></EllipseGeometry>
        <EllipseGeometry Center="40,140"></EllipseGeometry>
      </GeometryGroup>
    </Path.Data>
  </Path>
</Canvas>
```

Trying to code Bézier paths is a recipe for many thankless hours of trial-and-error computer coding. You're much more likely to draw your curves (and many other graphical elements) in a dedicated drawing program that has an export-to-XAML feature, or Microsoft Expression Blend.

Brushes

Many Silverlight elements support the concept of a background and foreground. Usually, the background is the surface of the element (as with the Canvas), while the foreground is the text (as with the TextBlock). In Silverlight, you set the color of these two areas (but not the content) using the Background and Foreground properties. The shape classes change this model a bit—instead of having Background or Foreground properties, they expose Fill and Stroke properties, which allow you to paint the interior region of the shape and the border around it.

It's natural to expect that the Background, Foreground, Fill, and Stroke properties would use some sort of color object. However, these properties actually use something much more versatile: a Brush object. That gives you the flexibility to fill your background and foreground content with a solid color (by using the SolidColorBrush) or something more exotic, like an image or gradient. Table 9 lists the brushes that Silverlight currently supports.

Table 9. *Brush Classes*

Name	Description
SolidColorBrush	Paints an area with a single color.
LinearGradientBrush	Paints an area using a gradient fill, a gradually shaded fill that changes from one color to another (and, optionally, to another and then another, and so on).
RadialGradientBrush	Paints an area using a radial gradient fill, which is similar to a linear gradient except it radiates out in a circular pattern starting from a center point.

Continued

Table 9. *Continued*

Name	Description
ImageBrush	Paints an area using an image that can be stretched, scaled, or tiled.
VideoBrush	Paints an area with the frames from a video. As the video plays, the brush changes, and the painted region is updated automatically. The VideoBrush works with Silverlight's media playback features.

Gradient Brushes

You've already seen an example of the RadialGradientBrush, where it was used to create a background for a Canvas. Both the RadialGradientBrush and LinearGradientBrush work in a similar way. They wrap a collection of GradientStop objects that set the colors in the gradient.

Often a gradient has two colors (allowing it to fade from one side to another with the LinearGradientBrush, or allowing it to radiate from a center point to an outer radius with the RadialGradientBrush). However, that's not a requirement. In fact, you can use as many colors as you want. The trick is setting the Offset property of each one to place it at a specific location in the gradient. The Offset value can range from 0 (at the start of the fill) to 1 (at the end).

For example, this gradient starts at yellow at the top-left corner and transitions through red, blue, and finally green at the bottom-right corner.

```
<Rectangle Width="150" Height="100">
  <Rectangle.Fill>
    <LinearGradientBrush>
      <GradientStop Color="Yellow" Offset="0.0" />
      <GradientStop Color="Red" Offset="0.25" />
      <GradientStop Color="Blue" Offset="0.75" />
      <GradientStop Color="Green" Offset="1.0" />
    </LinearGradientBrush>
  </Rectangle.Fill>
</Rectangle>
```

By changing the Offset values, you can modify this gradient so that it transitions to specific colors more quickly or more slowly. For example, if you want the colors to blend more slowly at the beginning and then end more quickly, you could give the offsets values of 0, 0.1, 0.3, and 1.

By default, the LinearGradientBrush paints its gradient diagonally, from the top-left corner of the fill region to the bottom-right. However, you might want to create a gradient that blends from top to bottom or side to side, or uses a different diagonal angle. You control these details using the StartPoint and EndPoint properties of the LinearGradientBrush. These properties allow you to choose the point where the first color begins to change and the point where the color change ends with the final color. (The area in between is blended gradually.) However, there's one quirk. The coordinates you use for the starting and ending point aren't real coordinates. Instead, the LinearGradientBrush assigns the point (0, 0) to the top-left corner and (1, 1) to the bottom-right corner of the area you want to fill, no matter how high and wide it actually is.

To create a top-to-bottom horizontal fill, you can use a start point of (0, 0) for the top-left corner, and an endpoint of (0, 1), which represents the bottom-left corner. To create a side-to-side vertical fill (with no slant), you can use a start point of (0, 0) and an endpoint of (1, 0) for the bottom-left corner, as shown here:

```
<Rectangle Width="150" Height="100">
  <Rectangle.Fill>
    <LinearGradientBrush StartPoint="0,0" EndPoint="1,0">
```

```
      ...
    </LinearGradientBrush>
  </Rectangle.Fill>
</Rectangle>
```

The RadialGradientBrush works similarly to the LinearGradientBrush. It also takes a sequence of colors with different offsets. As with the LinearGradientBrush, you can use as many colors as you want. The difference is how you place the gradient. To identify the point where the first color in the gradient starts, you use the GradientOrigin property. By default, it's (0.5, 0.5), which represents the middle of the fill region. The gradient radiates out from the starting point (set by StartPoint) in a circular fashion. Eventually, your gradient reaches the edge of an inner gradient circle (described by the Center, RadiusX, and RadiusY properties), where it ends. The area beyond the edge of the inner gradient circle and the outermost edge of the fill region is given a solid fill using the last color that's defined in the RadialGradientBrush.GradientStops collection.

Using Brushes to Fill Text

Remember, brushes aren't limited to shape drawing. You can substitute an exotic brush like LinearGradientBrush, RadialGradientBrush, ImageBrush, or VideoBrush anytime you would ordinarily use the SolidColorBrush. For example, Figure 18 shows an example of a TextBlock that has its Foreground property set to use the same multicolored LinearGradientBrush that was applied to the Rectangle element in the previous section.

Figure 18. *Using the LinearGradientBrush to set the TextBlock.Foreground property*

Transparency

In the examples you've considered so far, the shapes you've seen have been completely opaque. However, Silverlight supports true transparency. That means if you layer several elements on top of one another and give them all varying layers of transparency, you'll see exactly what you expect. At its simplest, this feature gives you the ability to create graphical backgrounds that "show through" the elements you place on top. At its most complex, this feature allows you to create multilayered animations and other effects.

There are several ways to make an element partly transparent:

- **Set the Opacity property**: Opacity is a fractional value from 0 to 1, where 1 is completely solid (the default) and 0 is completely transparent. The Opacity property is defined in the UIElement class (and the base Brush class), so it applies to all elements.

- **Use a semitransparent color**: Any color that has an alpha value less than 255 is semitransparent.

- **Set the OpacityMask property**: This allows you to make specific regions of an element transparent or partially transparent. For example, you can use it to fade a shape gradually into transparency.

The first two techniques are fairly straightforward. The OpacityMask property is a bit more involved, and it's demonstrated in the next example.

The OpacityMask property accepts any brush. The alpha channel of the brush determines where the transparency occurs.

Note Silverlight supports the ARGB color standard, which uses four values to describe every color. These four values (each of which ranges from 0 to 255) record the alpha, red, green, and blue components, respectively. The *alpha* component is a measure of how transparent the color is—0 is fully transparent and 255 is fully opaque. This is the only detail that matters when you're using a color (or an image that contains multiple colors) with the OpacityMask property.

Incidentally, Silverlight also supports a more complex standard called scRGB, which represents the four color components with floating point values. The scRGB standard uses the alpha channel to designate transparency in the same way as ARGB.

For example, if you use a SolidColorBrush that's set to a transparent color for your OpacityMask, your entire element will disappear. If you use a SolidColorBrush that's set to use a nontransparent color, your element will remain completely visible. The other details of the color (the red, green, and blue components) aren't important and are ignored when you set the OpacityMask property.

Using the OpacityMask with a SolidColorBrush doesn't make much sense because you can accomplish the same effect more easily with the Opacity property. However, OpacityMask becomes more useful when you use more exotic types of brushes, such as the LinearGradientBrush or RadialGradientBrush. Using a gradient that moves from a solid to a transparent color, you can create a transparency effect that fades in over the surface of your element.

For example, the following example creates two elements in the same place (their top-left corners are at the position (0, 0) in the Canvas). Based on the order of declaration, the blue rectangle will be superimposed over the image. However, the rectangle uses the OpacityMask property to gradually fade in transparency from left to right.

```
<Canvas ... >
  <Image Source="grandpiano.jpg"></Image>

  <Rectangle Fill="Blue" Width="300" Height="200">
    <Rectangle.OpacityMask>
      <LinearGradientBrush StartPoint="0,0" EndPoint="1,0">
        <GradientStop Offset="0" Color="Black"></GradientStop>
        <GradientStop Offset="1" Color="Transparent"></GradientStop>
      </LinearGradientBrush>
    </Rectangle.OpacityMask>
  </Rectangle>
</Canvas>
```

Figure 19 shows the result.

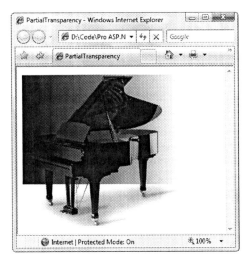

Figure 19. *A rectangle that fades from solid to transparent*

SILVERLIGHT CONTROLS

Silverlight graphics aren't just for static art. You can also use them to create controls. For example, if you use a Canvas to wrap a Rectangle in the background and place a TextBlock on top, you can create a surprisingly attractive button. Add a little event-handling logic and you'll have a dynamic button that changes its shading as your mouse moves over it.

In fact, the Silverlight 1.1 SDK includes samples that use this approach to create five common controls: a Button, a ScrollBar, a ScrollViewer (a scrollable region in which you can place content), a Slider, and a ListBox, all with a carefully shaded blue gradient fill. Eventually, these controls will be integrated into the core Silverlight assemblies, but they may change dramatically along the way. For now, you can include them with your own test projects. Just download the Silverlight 1.1 SDK from http://silverlight.net/GetStarted.

You may also be interested in third-party controls. One impressive example is GOA WinForms, which provides Silverlight elements that duplicate the basic controls from Windows Forms development. (There's also a version of GOA WinForms that provides the same set of controls for Flash applications.) You can find out more at http://community.netikatech.com/demos. Many third-party component developers are creating their own suites of Silverlight controls (one example is Sapphire by ComponentOne, at http://labs.componentone.com/Sapphire), and many developers are releasing their own open-source experiments (see http://tinyurl.com/39oaul for an ambitious example that includes a layout framework that emulates WPF).

Animation

Along with 2D drawing, animation is the other key capability of Silverlight 1.1. Animation allows you to create truly dynamic user interfaces. It's often used to apply effects—for example, icons that grow when you move over them, logos that spin, text that scrolls into view, and so on.

Animations are a core part of the Silverlight model. That means you don't need to use timers and event-handling code to put them into action. Instead, you can create them declaratively, configure them using one of a handful of classes, and put them into action without writing a single line of C# code.

Animation Basics

Silverlight animation is a scaled-down version of the WPF animation system. In order to understand Silverlight animation, you need to understand the following key rules:

- Silverlight performs time-based animation. Thus, you set the initial state, the final state, and the duration of your animation. Silverlight calculates the frame rate.

- Silverlight uses a property-based animation model. That means a Silverlight animation can do only one thing: modify the value of a property over an interval of time. This sounds like a significant limitation (and it many ways, it is), but there's a surprisingly large range of effects you can create by simply modifying properties.

- To animate a property, you need to have an animation class that supports its data type. For example, if you want to change a property that uses the double data type (which is one of the most common scenarios), you must use the DoubleAnimation class. If you want to modify the color that's used to paint the background of your Canvas, you need to use the ColorAnimation class.

   Silverlight has relatively few animation classes, so you're limited in the data types you can use. At present, you can use animations to modify properties with the following data types: double, Color, and Point.

   As a rule of thumb, the property-based animation is a great way to add dynamic effects to an otherwise ordinary application (like buttons that glow, pictures that expand when you move over them, and so on). However, if you need to use animations as part of the core purpose of your application and you want them to continue running over the lifetime of your application, you probably need something more flexible and more powerful. For example, if you're creating a basic arcade game or using complex physics calculations to model collisions, you'll need greater control over the animation. Unfortunately, Silverlight doesn't have an option for frame-based animation, so you'll be forced to create this sort of application the old-fashioned way—by looping endlessly, being careful to modify your visuals and check for user input after each iteration. You can see an example of this technique with the ball collision simulator at `http://bubblemark.com`.

Defining an Animation

Creating an animation is a multistep process. You need to create three separate ingredients: an animation object to perform your animation, a storyboard to manage your animation, and an event trigger to start your storyboard. In the following sections, you'll tackle each of these steps.

The Animation Class

There are actually two types of animation classes in Silverlight. Each type of animation uses a different strategy for varying a property value.

- **Linear interpolation**: With linear interpretation, the property value varies smoothly and continuously over the duration of the animation. Examples include DoubleAnimation, PointAnimation, and ColorAnimation.

- **Key frame animation**: With key frame animation, values can jump abruptly from one value to another, or they can combine jumps and periods of linear interpolation. Examples include ColorAnimationUsingKeyFrames, DoubleAnimationUsingKeyFrames, and PointAnimationUsingKeyFrames.

Here, you'll focus exclusively on the most commonly used animation class: the Double-Animation class. It uses linear interpolation to change a double from a starting value to its ending value.

Animations are defined using XAML markup. Although the animation classes aren't elements, they can still be created with the same XAML syntax. For example, here's the markup required to create a DoubleAnimation:

```
<DoubleAnimation From="160" To="300" Duration="0:0:5"></DoubleAnimation>
```

This animation lasts 5 seconds (as indicated by the Duration property, which takes a time value in the format Hours:Minutes:Seconds.FractionalSeconds). While the animation is running, it changes the target value from 160 to 300. Because the DoubleAnimation uses linear interpolation, this change takes place smoothly and continuously.

There's one important detail that's missing from this markup. The animation indicates how the property will be changed, but it doesn't indicate *what* property to use. This detail is supplied by another ingredient, which is represented by the Storyboard class.

The Storyboard Class

The storyboard manages the timeline of your animation. You can use a storyboard to group multiple animations, and it also has the ability to control the playback of animation—pausing it, stopping it, and changing its position. However, the most basic feature provided by the Storyboard class is its ability to point to a specific property and specific element using the TargetProperty and TargetName properties. In other words, the storyboard bridges the gap between your animation and the property you want to animate.

Here's how you might define a storyboard that applies a DoubleAnimation to the Width property of an element named rect:

```
<Storyboard x:Name="storyboard"
  Storyboard.TargetName="rect" Storyboard.TargetProperty="Width">
  <DoubleAnimation From="160" To="300" Duration="0:0:5"></DoubleAnimation>
</Storyboard>
```

Both TargetName and TargetProperty are attached properties. That means you can apply them directly to the animation, as shown here:

```
<Storyboard x:Name="storyboard">
  <DoubleAnimation
  Storyboard.TargetName="rect" Storyboard.TargetProperty="Width"
  From="160" To="300" Duration="0:0:5"></DoubleAnimation>
</Storyboard>
```

This syntax is more common, because it allows you to put several animations in the same storyboard but allow each animation to act on a different element and property.

If you give your storyboard a name (as in the previous example), you can interact with it in code. The Storyboard class includes four methods that let you manually control the animation: Begin(), Stop(), Pause(), and Resume(). However, if you simply want to start your animation in response to some event, there's an easier solution. You can wire this event directly to the BeginStoryboard action, as described in the next section.

The Event Trigger

Defining a storyboard and an animation are the first steps to creating an animation. To actually put this storyboard into action, you need an event trigger. An event trigger responds to an event by performing a storyboard action. The only storyboard action that Silverlight currently supports is BeginStoryboard, which starts a storyboard (and hence all the animations it contains).

The following example uses the Triggers collection of a Canvas to attach an animation to the Loaded event. When the Silverlight content is first rendered in the browser, and the Canvas element is loaded, the rectangle begins to grow. Five seconds later, its width has stretched from 160 pixels to 300.

```
<Canvas ... >
  <Canvas.Triggers>
    <EventTrigger RoutedEvent="Canvas.Loaded">
      <EventTrigger.Actions>
        <BeginStoryboard>
          <Storyboard>
            <DoubleAnimation Storyboard.TargetName="rect"
             Storyboard.TargetProperty="Width"
             From="160" To="300" Duration="0:0:5"></DoubleAnimation>
          </Storyboard>
        </BeginStoryboard>
      </EventTrigger.Actions>
    </EventTrigger>
  </Canvas.Triggers>

  <Rectangle Name="rect" Height="40" Width="160" Fill="Blue"
  Canvas.Left="10" Canvas.Top="10"></Rectangle>
</Canvas>
```

The Storyboard.TargetProperty property identifies the property you want to change (in this case, Width). If you don't supply a class name, the storyboard uses the parent element. If you want to set an attached property (for example, Canvas.Left or Canvas.Top), you need to wrap the entire property in brackets, like this:

```
<DoubleAnimation Storyboard.TargetProperty="(Canvas.Left)" ... />
```

If you want to use multiple animations in the same storyboard, you simply need to add more than one <Animation> element inside the <Storyboard> element. For example, you could use this technique to make the rectangle grow in width and height at the same time.

Starting an Animation with Code

The EventTrigger approach is an easy way to kick off an animation. However, in the current build, not all Silverlight events can be used as event triggers. The Loaded event is supported, but mouse-related events like MouseEnter, MouseLeave, and MouseMove are not.

If you want to start an animation in response to these events, you need to interact with the storyboard programmatically. Fortunately, it's easy. The first step is to move your storyboard out of the Triggers collection and place it in another collection of the same element: the Resources collection.

All Silverlight elements provide a Resources property, which holds a collection where you can store miscellaneous objects. The primary purpose of the Resources collection is to allow you to define objects in XAML that aren't elements, and so can't be placed into the visual layout of your content region. For example, you might want to declare a Brush object as a resource so it can be used by more than one element. Resources can be retrieved in your code or used elsewhere in your markup.

Here's an example that defines the rectangle-growing animation as a resource:

```
<Canvas x:Name="canvas" MouseLeftButtonDown="canvas_Click" ... >
  <Canvas.Resources>
    <Storyboard x:Name="growStoryboard">
      <DoubleAnimation Storyboard.TargetName="rect"
       Storyboard.TargetProperty="Width"
       Storyboard.TargetName="canvas"
```

```
        From="160" To="300" Duration="0:0:5"></DoubleAnimation>
    </Storyboard>
  </Canvas.Triggers>

  <Rectangle Name="rect" Height="40" Width="160" Fill="Blue"
   Canvas.Left="10" Canvas.Top="10"></Rectangle>
</Canvas>
```

Notice that it's now given a name, so you can manipulate it in your code. You'll also notice that you need to explicitly specify the Storyboard.TargetName property to connect it to the right element when you're using this approach.

Now you simply need to call the methods of the Storyboard object in an event handler in your Silverlight code-behind file. The methods you can use include Begin(), Stop(), Pause(), Resume, and Seek(), all of which are fairly self-explanatory.

```
private void canvas_Click(object o, EventArgs e)
{
    growStoryboard.Begin();
}
```

Configuring Animation Properties

To get the most out of your animations, you need to look a little closer at the base Animation class, which defines the properties that are provided by all animation classes. Table 10 describes them all.

Table 10. *Properties of the Animation Class*

Name	Description
From	Sets the starting values for your animation. In many situations, you won't set From. In this case, Silverlight uses the current value of your element. For example, if you didn't set the initial width in the growing rectangle example, it would start at whatever it is currently. This is particularly useful if you're animating a value that might be changed by other code or other animations. In this situation, you want the animation to start from the current value, not jump abruptly to a preset From value.
To	Sets the ending value for your animation. In some situations, you won't set From or To. In this case, the property returns to whatever initial value is set in the XAML markup. For example, you could use this technique to shrink the rectangle in the previous example back to its original size when it's clicked.
By	Instead of using To, you can use By to create a cumulative animation. By sets a number that will be added to the initial value. For example, if you replace the To value in the rectangle growing example with a By value of 10, the rectangle will grow 10 pixels wider than its current width over the course of the animation. If you run this animation every time the rectangle is clicked, it will continue to grow, and grow.
Duration	The length of time the animation runs, from start to finish, as a Duration object.
AutoReverse	If true, the animation will play out in reverse once it's complete, reverting to the original value. This also doubles the time the animation takes.
RepeatBehavior	Allows you to repeat an animation a specific number of seconds. Or, you can use Forever to repeat the animation endlessly.

Continued

Table 10. *Continued*

Name	Description
BeginTime	Sets a delay that will be added before the animation starts (as a TimeSpan). This delay is added to the total time, so a 5-second animation with a 5-second delay takes 10 seconds. BeginTime is useful when synchronizing different animations that start at the same time but should apply their effects in sequence.
SpeedRatio	Increases or decreases the speed of the animation. Ordinarily, SpeedRatio is 1. If you increase it, the animation completes more quickly (for example, a SpeedRatio of 5 completes five times faster). If you decrease it, the animation is slowed down (for example, a SpeedRatio of 0.5 takes twice as long). You can change the duration of your animation for an equivalent result. The SpeedRatio is not taken into account when applying the BeginTime delay.
FillBehavior	Determines what happens when the animation ends. Usually, it keeps the property fixed at the ending value (FillBehavior.HoldEnd), but you can also choose to return it to its original value (FillBehavior.Stop).

An Interactive Animation Example

In the previous example, you used animation to alter an element when it first appears. However, in most applications, animations will be triggered by another event, such as a mouse movement or a mouse click.

The following example demonstrates a slightly more realistic use of animation, which is shown in Figure 20. It begins with a content region that's filled with irregularly shaped rectangles. When you click a rectangle, it begins to fall toward the bottom of the Canvas, and simultaneously begins to change color. When you click another rectangle, the first animation stops and that rectangle begins to fall.

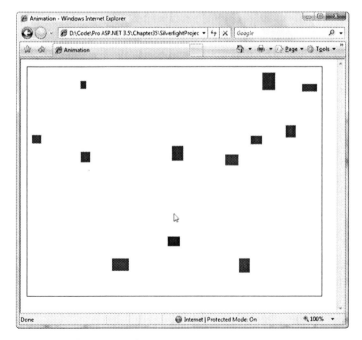

Figure 20. *Falling rectangles*

This animation example is simple, but it demonstrates several of the subtle concepts in Silverlight animation.

The markup for this example defines a single storyboard. This storyboard isn't placed in a Triggers collection, because initially it isn't wired up to any specific rectangle. Instead, it's placed in the Canvas.Resources collection so it can be retrieved by your code when needed.

```
<Canvas ... >
  <Canvas.Resources>
    <Storyboard x:Name="fallingSquareStoryboard">
      <DoubleAnimation
        Storyboard.TargetProperty="(Canvas.Top)"
        To="400" Duration="0:0:2" />
      <ColorAnimation Storyboard.TargetProperty="Rectangle.Fill.Color"
        To="Blue" Duration="0:0:2" />
    </Storyboard>
  </Canvas.Resources>
</Canvas>
```

This storyboard wraps two animations: a DoubleAnimation that moves the rectangle, and a ColorAnimation that changes its color. The ColorAnimation uses linear interpolation, which means it will progressively blend the color from its initial value (in this example, red) to its final value (blue).

You'll also notice that the Canvas doesn't contain any other elements. That's because this example uses a more flexible approach—it generates the rectangles dynamically. When the Canvas is loaded, it creates 12 rectangles of random size, at random locations. It wires the MouseLeftButton-Down event of each one to the same event handler.

```
public void Page_Loaded(object o, EventArgs e)
{
    // Required to initialize variables
    InitializeComponent();

    // Generate some rectangles.
    Random rand = new Random();
    for (int i = 0; i < 12; i++)
    {
        Rectangle rect = new Rectangle();
        rect.Fill = new SolidColorBrush(Colors.Red);

        // Size and place it randomly.
        rect.Width = rand.Next(10, 40);
        rect.Height = rand.Next(10, 40);
        rect.SetValue<double>(Canvas.TopProperty,
          rand.Next((int)this.Height / 2));
        rect.SetValue<double>(Canvas.LeftProperty,
          rand.Next((int)this.Width));

        // Handle clicks.
        rect.MouseLeftButtonDown += rect_Click;

        // Give it a unique name, which is required for animation.
        rect.SetValue<string>(Rectangle.NameProperty, "rect" + i.ToString());
```

```
            // Add it to the Canvas.
            this.Children.Add(rect);
        }
    }
```

When a rectangle is clicked, there are two steps that need to be performed. The animation for the current rectangle needs to be halted (by calling the Storyboard.Stop() method), and the existing storyboard needs to be attached to the new rectangle.

However, there's a trick here. Animations don't actually change the underlying value of a property, they simply override it temporarily. When the end of an animation is reached, the property is held indefinitely at its final value (unless you've set the FillBehavior property of the animation class to FillBehavior.Stop). But in this example, the animation needs to be repeatedly stopped. If you don't take any extra steps, each time you stop the animation of a falling rectangle, its position will be reset to its original value, meaning it will "jump" back up to the top of the Canvas.

The solution is to retrieve the current value of the Canvas.Top property for the rectangle, then stop the animation, and then set the animated value. This last step moves the rectangle to its most recent animated position. The result is that every time you click a new rectangle, the rectangle that was falling previously halts in its tracks, but remains in the same position.

Here's the code that implements this design:

```
// Keep track of the rectangle that's being animated.
private Rectangle currentlyFallingRectangle;

private void rect_Click(object o, EventArgs e)
{
    // Retrieve the Storyboard.
    Storyboard sb = (Storyboard)this.FindName("fallingSquareStoryboard");
    if (currentlyFallingRectangle != null)
    {
        // Stop the current animation and move the rectangle
        // to its current position.
        double top =
          (double)currentlyFallingRectangle.GetValue(Canvas.TopProperty);
        sb.Stop();
        currentlyFallingRectangle.SetValue<double>(Canvas.TopProperty, top);
    }

    // Get the rectangle that was clicked.
    currentlyFallingRectangle = (Rectangle)o;

    // Start the animation for the new rectangle.
    sb.SetValue<string>(Storyboard.TargetNameProperty,
      currentlyFallingRectangle.Name);
    sb.Begin();
}
```

Although the Canvas.Top property is set manually after the animation is stopped, the color is not. As a result, the rectangle reverts to its initial blue color as soon as another rectangle starts falling.

There's another interesting quirk in this example. The animation always uses the same duration (2 seconds). However, the square you click may be close to the bottom or far from the bottom. As a result, squares closer to the bottom will fall more slowly, and squares farther from the bottom will fall faster.

In this example, there's only one storyboard at work at a time. It's reasonable to ask if you could create a similar example where every rectangle you click continues falling. This is possible, but a different design is required.

In the current build of Silverlight 1.1, Storyboard objects can't be fully configured programmatically. Thus, you need to have the storyboard and animations you need defined in your XAML. This is obviously a challenge if you're creating elements dynamically, and don't know how many storyboards you'll use. The solution is to create a custom control that has its own animation behavior. To implement this design in the previous example, you'd create a custom rectangle that has its own XAML template. This XAML would specify the animation that should be used for that rectangle. Thus, every time you create an instance of this custom control, it comes pre-wired with the animation support. Unfortunately, this more modular design takes a fair bit more code, and it's out of the scope of this article. However, if you're interested in learning more, check out the Silverlight Balloons example at http://tinyurl.com/398qf4. It illustrates this principle neatly with an endless sequence of rising balloons (each of which is an instance of a custom Balloon control).

Transforms

As you've already learned, Silverlight animations work by modifying the value of a property. Elements have several properties that can be usefully changed. For example, you can use Canvas.Left and Canvas.Top to move an element around. Or, you can alter the Opacity setting to make an element fade into or out of view. However, it's not immediately clear how you can perform more exciting alterations, like rotations.

The secret is *transforms*. A transform is an object that alters the way a shape or other element is drawn by shifting the coordinate system it uses. You can use transforms to stretch, rotate, skew, and otherwise manipulate the shapes, images, and text in your Silverlight user interface. Transforms are useful for getting the right shape you want, but they're even more interesting when you're animating. By animating a property in a transform, you can rotate a shape, move it from one place to another, or warp it dynamically.

Table 11 lists the transforms that are supported in Silverlight.

Table 11. *Transform Classes*

Name	Description	Important Properties
TranslateTransform	Displaces your coordinate system by some amount. This transform is useful if you want to draw the same shape in different places.	X, Y
RotateTransform	Rotates your coordinate system. The shapes you draw normally are turned around a center point you choose.	Angle, CenterX, CenterY
ScaleTransform	Scales your coordinate system up or down so that your shapes are drawn smaller or larger. You can apply different degrees of scaling in the X and Y dimensions, thereby stretching or compressing your shape.	ScaleX, ScaleY, CenterX, CenterY
SkewTransform	Warps your coordinate system by slanting it a number of degrees. For example, if you draw a square, it becomes a parallelogram.	AngleX, AngleY, CenterX, CenterY

Continued

Table 11. *Continued*

Name	Description	Important Properties
MatrixTransform	Modifies your coordinate system using matrix multiplication with the matrix you supply. This is the most complex option—it requires some mathematical skill.	Matrix
TransformGroup	Combines multiple transforms so they can all be applied at once. The order in which you apply transformations is important—it affects the final result. For example, rotating a shape (with RotateTransform) and then moving it (with TranslateTransform) sends the shape off in a different direction than if you move it and *then* rotate it.	N/A

Technically, all transforms use matrix math to alter the coordinates of your shape. However, using prebuilt transforms such as TranslateTransform, RotateTransform, ScaleTransform, and SkewTransform is far simpler than using the MatrixTransform and trying to work out the right matrix for the operation you want to perform. When you perform a series of transforms with TransformGroup, Silverlight fuses your transforms together into a single MatrixTransform, ensuring optimal performance.

Using a Transform

To transform an element, you set its RenderTransform property with the transform object you want to use. Depending on the transform object you're using, you'll need to fill in different properties to configure it, as detailed in Table 11.

For example, if you're rotating a shape, you need to use the RotateTransform and supply the angle in degrees. Here's an example that rotates a square clockwise by 25 degrees:

```
<Rectangle Width="80" Height="10" Stroke="Blue" Fill="Yellow"
 Canvas.Left="100" Canvas.Top="100">
  <Rectangle.RenderTransform>
    <RotateTransform Angle="25" />
  </Rectangle.RenderTransform>
</Rectangle>
```

When you rotate a shape in this way, you rotate it about the shape's origin (the top-left corner). If you want to rotate a shape around a different point, you can use the handy RenderTransformOrigin property. This property sets the center point using a proportional coordinate system that stretches from 0 to 1 in both dimensions. In other words, the point (0, 0) is designated as the top-left corner, and (1, 1) is the bottom-right corner. (If the shape region isn't square, the coordinate system is stretched accordingly.)

With the help of the RenderTransformOrigin property, you can rotate any shape around its center point using markup like this:

```
<Rectangle Width="80" Height="10" Stroke="Blue" Fill="Yellow"
 Canvas.Left="100" Canvas.Top="100" RenderTransformOrigin="0.5,0.5">
  <Rectangle.RenderTransform>
    <RotateTransform Angle="25" />
  </Rectangle.RenderTransform>
</Rectangle>
```

This works because the point (0.5, 0.5) designates the center of the shape, regardless of its size.

Tip You can use values greater than 1 or less than 0 when setting the RenderTransformOrigin property to designate a point that appears outside the bounding box of your shape. For example, you can use this technique with a RotateTransform to rotate a shape in a large arc around a very distant point, such as (5, 5).

Animating a Transform

To use a transform in animation, the first step is to define the transform. (An animation can change an existing transform but not create a new one.) For example, imagine you want to allow a rectangle to rotate. This requires RotateTransform:

```
<Rectangle x:Name="rect" Width="80" Height="50" Stroke="Blue" Fill="Yellow"
 Canvas.Left="100" Canvas.Top="100" RenderTransformOrigin="0.5,0.5">
  <Rectangle.RenderTransform>
    <RotateTransform></RotateTransform>
  </Rectangle.RenderTransform>
</Rectangle>
```

Now here's a storyboard that makes the rectangle rotate when the mouse moves over it. It uses the target property (UIElement.RenderTransform).Angle—in other words, it reads the RenderTransform property of the Rectangle and modifies the Angle property of the RotateTransform object that's defined there. The fact that the RenderTransform property can hold a variety of different transform objects, each with different properties, doesn't cause a problem. As long as you're using a transform that has an angle property, this trigger will work.

```
<Rectangle x:Name="rect" Width="80" Height="50" Stroke="Blue" Fill="Yellow"
 Canvas.Left="100" Canvas.Top="100" RenderTransformOrigin="0.5,0.5"
 MouseEnter="rect_Enter">
  <Rectangle.RenderTransform>
    <RotateTransform></RotateTransform>
  </Rectangle.RenderTransform>
  <Rectangle.Resources>
    <Storyboard x:Name="rotateStoryboard">
      <DoubleAnimation
        Storyboard.TargetName="rect"
        Storyboard.TargetProperty="(UIElement.RenderTransform).Angle"
        To="360" Duration="0:0:0.8" RepeatBehavior="Forever"></DoubleAnimation>
    </Storyboard>
  </Rectangle.Resources>
</Rectangle>
```

Finally, an event handler starts the storyboard:

```
private void rect_Enter(object o, EventArgs e)
{
    rotateStoryboard.Begin();
}
```

The rectangle rotates one revolution every 0.8 seconds and continues rotating perpetually. While the rectangle is rotating, it's still completely usable—for example, it still raises the MouseLeftButtonDown event if you click it.

To stop the rotation, you can use a second trigger that responds to the MouseLeave event. At this point, you could call the Storyboard.Stop() method, but this will cause the button to jump back to its original orientation in one step. A better approach is to start a *second* animation that replaces the first. Here's how the second animation is defined:

```
<Storyboard x:Name="revertStoryboard">
  <DoubleAnimation
   Storyboard.TargetName="rect"
   Storyboard.TargetProperty="(UIElement.RenderTransform).Angle"
   To="0" Duration="0:0:0.2"></DoubleAnimation>
</Storyboard>
```

This animation seamlessly rotates the rectangle back to its original orientation in a snappy 0.2 seconds. You can place this storyboard in the same Rectangle.Resources collection as the first animation. All you need to do is attach an event handler to the Rectangle.MouseLeave event that runs the storyboard:

```
private void rect_Leave(object o, EventArgs e)
{
    revertStoryboard.Begin();
}
```

■**Tip** You can easily use transforms in combination. In fact, it's easy—you simply need to use the TransformGroup to set the RenderTransform property. You can nest as many transforms as you need inside the TransformGroup.

Summary

In this article, you took a thorough look at Silverlight, a new platform that's modeled after two other technologies: .NET and WPF.

Silverlight is evolving rapidly. In a matter of months, there will be further releases with more controls and new features. At present, Silverlight still doesn't provide enough features for anything except highly customized and highly graphical applications. The lack of basics (like a text-entry control) makes it of less interest to business developers.

Although it's still a bit too early to assess Silverlight's browser plug-in and its performance on other browser and operating systems, there's reason to expect the best. Silverlight is one of Microsoft's most highly anticipated new technologies, often inspiring more developer interest than any other release since .NET 1.0. Developers who learn the Silverlight model now will have a head start in mastering more mature future versions.

If you've decided to embark on a Silverlight project, the best starting point is to look at some at the existing samples on the Web. They are the best tutorials to learn how developers have tackled the limitations of the current Silverlight platform, such as creating custom controls, showing separate "screens," performing background work, and managing the lifetime of the application. You can find a set of excellent samples with complete source code at http://silverlight.net/community/ gallerydetail.aspx?cat=2. For more information about Silverlight 1.1 controls that you might want to use, refer to the "Silverlight Controls" mentioned earlier.

Printed in the United States
109053LV00005B/1-4/A

9 781590 599396